The
Princeton
Review

Crash Course
for the New
GRE

4th Edition

Neill Seltzer and Wendy Voelkle

PrincetonReview.com

Random House, Inc. New York

Princeton Review Publishing, Inc.
111 Speen Street
Suite 550
Framingham, MA 01701

E-mail: editorialsupport@review.com

Published in the United States by Random House, Inc., New York, and simultaneously in Canada by Random House of Canada Limited, Toronto.

ISBN 978-0-375-42822-7
ISSN 1545-620X
Editor: Laura Braswell
Production Editor: Stephanie Tantum
Production Coordinator: Deborah A. Silvestrini

Printed in the United States of America on partially recycled paper.

10   9   8   7   6   5   4   3   2   1

Fourth Edition

CONTENTS

General Book Budget

11/20/11

PART I

INTRODUCTION

ORIENTATION

WHAT IS *CRASH COURSE FOR THE NEW GRE*?

Crash Course for the New GRE is just what it sounds like—a quick, but thorough, guide to the essential fundamentals of the new GRE. It includes helpful techniques for nailing as many question as possible, even if you don't have a lot of time to prepare. *Crash Course for the New GRE* will give you an overview of the new test, exposure to all question types, and loads of helpful advice, but it is not a comprehensive study guide for the GRE. Go to Princetonreview.com and take a full-length online practice test to find out your starting score. If you need significant score improvements or more intensive review of any of the subject matter you encounter, try *Cracking the New GRE* (which has been revised for the GRE test changes) or *1,014 Practice Questions for the New GRE.*

WHAT IS THE GRE?

The Graduate Record Exam (GRE) is a multiple-choice aptitude test intended for applicants to graduate schools. It definitely does not measure your intelligence, nor, ironically, does it measure your quality as a candidate. All it really measures is how well you handle standardized tests. Luckily, this is a skill you can improve with practice.

You will receive a math score, a verbal score, and an analytic writing score. These correspond to the three types of sections you will see on the test. Section by section, here's how the test breaks down:

SECTION	NUMBER OF QUESTIONS	ALLOTTED TIME
Analytic Writing (one section with two separately timed essays)	One "Analyze an Issue" essay and one "Analyze an Argument" essay	30 minutes per essay
Verbal Reasoning (x2)	20 Questions	30 minute per section
Quantitative Reasoning (x2)	20 Questions	35 minutes per section
Break		10 minutes
Experimental	20 Questions	30/35 minutes
Research	Varies	Varies

Your essay sections will always come first. These are two back-to-back essays, with 30 minutes each to write. After the essays, you will have two of your five multiple-choice sections, and then you get your one and only proper break after section three. Most students will see five multi-question sections, either two verbal and three math or three verbal and two math. Two verbal sections and two math sections will always count. The extra section is an experimental one. It may be math or verbal. It will look just like the other sections, but it will not count. These five sections, including the experimental, could occur in any order. There is no way to know which section is experimental. You will have a one-minute break between each of these sections.

Occasionally, you will get a research section in place of the experimental section. If so, the research section will come last, and it will be identified as a research section. The test will specifically say that the section does not count toward your score. If you see one of these, your test is over, and your first four multi-question sections counted.

MATH QUESTION TYPES

Quantitative Comparison—Quant comps, for short, give you information in two columns. Your job is to decide if the values in the two quantities are the same, if one is larger, or if it is impossible to say. Tip: If there are no variables in either quantity, eliminate answer choice (D).

Problem Solving—These are the typical five-answer multiple-choice questions you probably remember from the SAT. You must correctly select one of the five answer choices to get credit. Tip: They've given you the answers. One of them is correct. Use the answer choices to help solve the problem.

Select All That Apply—This is a new twist on the old multiple-choice question. In this case you may have three or up to eight answer choices, and one or more will be correct. You must select all of the correct answer choices to get credit. **Tip:** The answer choices are generally in chronological order, so start in the middle and look to eliminate as many wrong answer choices as possible.

Numeric Entry—Alas, these are not multiple choice. It is your job to come up with your own number and type it into the box provided. For fractions, you will be given two boxes, and you must fill in the top and the bottom separately. Tip: You don't have to reduce your fractions. The computer reads $\frac{44}{88}$ the same as $\frac{1}{2}$, so save yourself a step.

The Calculator

The new GRE now provides an onscreen calculator. Like the calculator you might find on your computer, this one will add, subtract, multiply, divide, and find a square root. It also has a transfer number button that allows you to transfer the number on the calculator screen directly to the box on a Numeric Entry question. This button will be grayed out on a multiple-choice question.

Since we all use calculators in our daily life, it's about time they provided one on the GRE. Certainly this should cut down on basic calculation errors and save a bit of time on questions that involve things like averages or percentages. The GRE, however, is not generally a test of your ability to do large calculations, nor is the calculator a replacement for your brain. The test makers will look for ways to test your analytic skills, often making the calculator an unnecessary temptation, or, at times, even a liability. Be particularly careful of questions that ask you to provide answers in a specific format. A question may ask you to provide an answer rounded to the nearest tenth, for example. If your calculator gives you an answer of 3.48, and you transfer that number, you will get the question wrong. Or a question may ask you for a percent and will have the percent symbol next to the answer box. In this case they are looking for a whole number. Depending upon how you solve the problem on your calculator, you may end up with an answer of .25 for 25%. If you enter the decimal, you will get the question wrong.

Here are a few tips for when to use and when not to use your calculator on the GRE:

Good Calculator

- Multiplying two- and three- digit numbers
- Finding percentages or averages
- Working questions involving Order of Operations (The calculator will understand Order of Operations. If you type in $3 + 5 \times 6$, it will know to prioritize multiplication over addition, for example.)
- Working with decimals

Bad Calculator

- Converting fractions to decimals in order to avoid working with fractions (better that you know the rules and are comfortable with fractions)

- Attempting to solve large exponents, square roots, or other calculation-heavy operations. There is almost always a faster way to do the problem.

- Adding or subtracting negative numbers if you're not sure of the rules

- Solving charts problems with multiple questions. Write all information down on your scratch paper and label everything. Information you find on one problem might help on another. If you do everything on your calculator, you will have to recalculate.

VERBAL QUESTION TYPES

Text Completion—These used to be Sentence Completion, but now they've gotten longer, and you must work with each blank independently. Questions may have between one and five sentences and one to three blanks. A one-blank question will have five answer choices. A two- or three-blank question will have three choices per blank. You must select the correct word for each blank to get credit for the question.

Sentence Equivalence—These look like Sentence Completion questions but there is one blank and six answer choices. You must select two answer choices from the six provided. The correct answers will each complete the sentence and keep the meaning the same.

Reading Comprehension—Reading Comp supplies you with a passage and then asks you questions about the information in the passage, the author's intent, or the structure.

There are three distinct question types that could occur here:

- **Multiple Choice**—You must select one correct answer from five choices.

- **Select All That Apply**—These questions used to number three choices with roman numerals and you had to pick I, I and II only, and so on. Now you simply select the correct answer or answers from a group of three choices.

- **Select in Passage**—You will be asked to click on an actual sentence in the passage. You may click on any one word to select the whole sentence. Only one sentence is correct. These questions will occur primarily on short passages. If they occur in a long passage, the question will specify a particular paragraph.

WHAT DOES A GRE SCORE LOOK LIKE?

You will receive separate Verbal and Quantitative scores, each on a scale that runs from 130 to 170 in one-point increments. Your Analytical Writing score is on a scale of 0 to 6 in half-point increments. For example:

YOUR SCORES:

163 QUANT
158 VERBAL
5.5 ANALYTIC

Where Does the GRE Come From?

Like most standardized tests in this country, the GRE is published by ETS, a big, tax-exempt private company in New Jersey. ETS publishes the GRE under the sponsorship of the Graduate Record Examinations Board, an organization affiliated with the Association of Graduate Schools and the Council of Graduate Schools in the United States.

The GRE isn't written by distinguished professors, renowned scholars, or graduate-school admissions officers. For the most part, it's written by ordinary ETS employees, sometimes with freelance help from local graduate students. There's no reason to be intimidated by these people.

Why Should I Listen to The Princeton Review?

We monitor the GRE. Our teaching methods for cracking it were developed through exhaustive analysis of all available GREs and careful research into the methods by which standardized tests are constructed. Our focus is on the basic concepts that will enable you to attack any problem, strip it down to its essential components, and solve it in as little time as possible.

GRE Facts

You can schedule a test session ($140 at the time of publication) online, by phone, or by mail. In general, web registration is the quickest and the easiest since you can see a calendar and test center locations. Log on to www.GRE.org and click on "Register for the Test" under "General Test." If registering by phone, call (800) 473-2255. ETS accepts all major credit cards.

The GRE website will answer most questions, including guidelines for disability accommodations, international testing, as well as test center locations and dates. For additional questions, call ETS directly at (609) 771-7670.

WHAT THE NEW GRE LOOKS LIKE

The problem you're working on will be in the middle of the screen. If there is additional information, such as a chart or graph or passage, it will be on a split screen either above the question or to the left of it. If the entire chart[s] or passage or additional information does not fit on the split screen, there will be a scroll bar.

Questions with only a single answer will have an oval selection field. To select an answer, just click on the oval. A question with the potential for multiple correct answers will have square answer fields. An x appears in the square when you select the answer choice. At the bottom of the screen, under the question, there may be some basic directions, such as "Click on your choice."

A read-out of the time remaining in the section will be displayed in the upper-right corner. Next to it is a button that allows you to hide the time. No matter what, the time will return and will begin to blink on and off when you have five minutes remaining on a particular section. At the top center the display will tell you which question number you are working on, out of the total number of questions. The top of the screen will also contain the following five buttons:

Exit Section—This button indicates that you are done with a particular section. Should you finish a section early, you can use this button to get to the next section. Once you've exited a section, however, you cannot return to it. Note that the two essays are considered a single section. If you use this button after your first essay, you will have skipped the second essay.

Review—This button brings up a review screen. The review screen will indicate which questions you've seen, which ones you've answered, and which ones you've marked. From the review screen you can return to the question you've just left, or you can return to an earlier question.

Mark—The mark button is just what it looks like. You may mark a question for whatever reason you choose. This does not answer the question. You may mark a question whether you've answered it or not. Marked questions will appear as marked on the review screen.

Help—The help button will drop you into the help tab for the particular question type you are working on. From there, there are three additional tabs. One gives you "Section Directions." This is an overview of the section, including the number of questions, the amount of time allotted, and a brief description of the function of ovals versus boxes. The second is "General Directions" on timing and breaks, test information, and the repeater policy. The last additional tab is "Testing Tools." This is an overview of each of the buttons available to you during a section. Note that the help button will not stop the clock. The clock continues to run even if you are clicking around and reading directions.

Back/Next—These two buttons get you on to the next question or back to the prior question. You can continue to click these as many times as you like until you get to the beginning or end of the section. If you return to a question you have answered, the question will display your answer.

We will talk more about strategies for pacing on the test and ways to use the mark and review buttons. You should never need the help button. Ideally you will be familiar enough with the functions of the test that you don't have to spend valuable test time reading directions.

> You should never need the help button. Be familiar with the testing tools before you go into the text.

How the New GRE Works

The new test is adaptive by section. Your score is determined by the number of questions you get right and their difficulty level. On the first verbal section, the test will give you a mix of medium questions. Based upon the percentage of questions you get right on that first section, the computer will select questions for the second section. The more you get right on the first section, the harder the questions you will see on the second section, but more potential points you could get.

Everything is determined by the number of questions you get right, not by the number of questions you answer. Accuracy, therefore, will always trump speed. It makes no sense to worry about the clock and rush through a section if your accuracy suffers as a result.

Real Tests

You bought *Crash Course for the New GRE* because you don't have a lot of time to prepare, and you want the basics. But you still need real GRE questions on which to practice. The only source of real GREs is the publisher of the test, ETS. Therefore, if you have the time, we recommend that you download GRE POWERPREP® Software—Test Preparation for the General Test, which includes GRE questions presented in the CAT mode from www.gre.org. You will also receive a copy on CD-ROM when you register for the GRE.

Stay Current

The information in this book is accurate right now, and will be updated yearly. However, the publishing business is such that if the test changed tomorrow, the book might be a little behind. For the most current information possible, visit ETS's website at www.gre.org, or our website at PrincetonReview.com.

GENERAL
STRATEGY

TAKE THE EASY TEST FIRST!

On the GRE, there are questions and there are questions. Some are a breeze, while others will have you tearing your hair out. The new GRE has been constructed so that you can answer questions in any order you like, and the questions you get on the second section will depend upon the number of questions you get right on the first section. You can maximize that number by starting with the questions you like. Remember that every question counts equally toward your score. As you work through a section, if you see a question you don't like or understand, skip it. If you see one that looks as if it will take a long time, skip it. If you love geometry, but hate algebra, do all of the geometry questions first and leave the algebra questions for last.

> Unless you are shooting for a 700 (on the old scale) or higher, you should NOT attempt to answer every single question.

As long as you are going to run out of time, you might as well run out of time on the questions you are least likely to get right. By leaving time-consuming and difficult questions for the end, you will be able to get to more questions overall, and get more of them right. Do not mark questions you skip; we will use the mark function for something else. Just click "Next" and move on to the next question. The review screen will tell you which questions you have and have not answered.

Note: There is no guessing penalty on the GRE. They don't take points away for a wrong answer. When you get to the two-minute mark, therefore, stop what you're doing and bubble in any unanswered questions.

ANSWER QUESTIONS IN STAGES

Any time you practice for a test, you end up getting a few wrong. Later, when reviewing these questions, you end up smacking your forehead and asking yourself, "What was I thinking?" Alternately, you may find a problem utterly impossible to solve the first time around, only to look at it later and realize that it was actually quite easy, you just misread the question or missed a key piece of information.

On a four-hour test, your brain is going to get tired. When your brain gets tired, you're going make mistakes. Typically these mistakes consist of misreadings or simple calculation errors. A misread question or a calculation error will completely change the way you see the problem. Unfortunately, once you see a question wrong, it is almost impossible to un-see it and see it correctly. As long as you stay with that question, you will continue to see it wrong every time. Meanwhile, the clock is ticking and you're not getting any closer to the answer. We call this La La Land. Once you're in La La Land, it is very difficult to get out.

On the flip side, once you've spotted the error, solving the problem correctly is often quick work. A question that bedeviled you for minutes on end in the middle of a test may appear to be appallingly obvious when viewed in the comfort of a post-test review. The trick is to change the way you see the question while you still have the opportunity to fix it.

Step 1—Recognize La La Land.

Step 2—Distract your brain.

Step 3—See the problem with fresh eyes and fix it.

Step 1—Recognize La La Land. This is often the hardest part of the process. The more work you've put into a problem, the more difficult it is to walk away from it. Once you get off track on a problem, however, any additional work you invest in that problem is wasted effort. No problem on the GRE, if you understand what's being asked, should ever take more than a minute or two to solve. If you go over two minutes, you're off track. Get out. If you find yourself working too hard, or plowing through reams of calculations, you are off track. Get out. Here are a few signs that you are in La La Land:

a. You've found an answer but it is not one of the choices they've given you.

b. You have half a page of calculations, but are no closer to an answer.

c. You've spent more than four minutes on a problem.

d. Your hand is not moving.

e. You're down to two answer choices, and you would swear on your life that both are correct.

f. There is smoke coming out of your ears.

g. You're beginning to wonder if they made a mistake when they wrote the question.

If you find yourself in any of these situations, you are in La La Land. Stop what you're doing and get out. You've got better things to do with your time than sitting around wrestling with this question.

Step 2—Distract your brain. When you find yourself faced with an immovable object, walk away. Think of it this way: You could spend four minutes on a question even when you know you're stuck, or you could walk away and spend those same four minutes on three other easier questions and get them all right. Why throw good minutes after bad? Whether they realize it or not, ETS has actually designed the test to facilitate this process. This is where the Mark button comes into play. If you don't like a problem or don't know how to solve it, just skip it. If you start a problem and get stuck, mark it and move to the next question before you waste too much time. Do two other problems, three tops, and then return to the problem that was giving you trouble.

When you walk away from a problem, you're not walking away entirely; you're just parking it on the back burner. Your brain is still chewing on it, but it's processing in the background while you work on something else. Sometimes your best insights occur when your attention is pointed elsewhere. Walk away from a problem early and often. You want to always have questions to use to distract your brain. If you don't walk away, and you take the test in order, you will not have questions available at the tail end of a section. On some difficult problems you may walk away more than once. It is OK to take two or three runs at a hard problem.

Step 3—See the problem with fresh eyes and fix it. You use other problems to distract your brain so that you can see a troublesome problem with fresh eyes. You can help this process out by trying to read the question differently when you return to it. Use your finger on the screen to force yourself to read the problem word for word. Are there different ways to express the information? Can you use the answer choices to help? Can you paraphrase the answer choices as well? If the path to the right answer is not clear on a second viewing, walk away again. Why stick with a problem you don't know how to solve?

The Amazing Power of POE

There are roughly four times as many wrong answers as there are right answers; it's often easier to identify the wrong answers than it is to identify the right ones. POE stands for Process of Elimination. On hard questions, spend your time looking for and eliminating wrong answers. They are easier and quicker to find.

The simple act of eliminating wrong answers, something anyone can do on any question, will raise your score. Why? Because every time you're able to eliminate an incorrect choice on a GRE question, you improve your odds of finding the best answer. The more incorrect choices you eliminate, the better your odds. Don't be afraid to arrive at ETS's answer indirectly. You'll be avoiding the traps laid in your path by the test writers—traps that are designed to catch unwary test takers who try to approach the problems directly.

If you guessed blindly on a five-choice GRE problem, you would have one chance in five of picking ETS's answer. Eliminate one incorrect choice, and your chances improve to one in four. Eliminate three, and you have a fifty-fifty chance of earning points by guessing. Get the picture? Why not improve your odds?

> Note: Especially on verbal questions, if you're not sure what a word in an answer choice means, don't eliminate that choice. It might be the answer! Only eliminate answers you know are wrong.

The "Best" Answer

The instructions on the GRE tell you to select the "best" answer to each question. ETS calls them "best" answers, or the "credited responses," instead of "correct" answers, to protect itself from the complaints of test takers who might be tempted to quarrel with ETS's judgment. You have to pick from the choices ETS gives you, and sometimes you might not like any of them. Your job is to find the one answer for which ETS gives credit.

Use That Paper!

For POE to work, it's crucial that you keep track of what choices you're eliminating. By crossing out a clearly incorrect choice, you permanently eliminate it from consideration. If you don't cross it out, you'll keep considering it. Crossing out incorrect choices can make it much easier to find the credited response, because there will be fewer places where it can hide. But how can you cross anything out on a computer screen?

By using your scratch paper! On the GRE, the answer choices have empty bubbles next to them, but in this book, we'll refer to them as (A), (B), (C), (D), and (E). Each time you see a question, get in the habit of immediately writing down A, B, C, D, E on your scratch paper.

A	A	A	A
B	B	B	B
C	C	C	C
D	D	D	D
E	E	E	E
A	A	A	A
B	B	B	B
C	C	C	C
D	D	D	D
E	E	E	E

Mark up at least a couple of pages (front and back) like this before the test officially starts. This will give you a bunch of distinct work areas per page, which will be especially helpful for the Math section. You don't want to get confused when your work from one question runs into your work from a previous question.

You then can physically cross off choices that you're eliminating. Do it every time you do a GRE question, whether in this book or elsewhere. Get used to writing on scratch paper instead of near the question, because you won't be able to write near the question on test day.

Don't Do Anything in Your Head

Besides eliminating incorrect answers, there are many other ways to use scratch paper to solve questions; you're going to learn them all. Just remember: Even if you're tempted to try to solve questions in your head, even if you think that writing things down on your scratch paper is a waste of time, you're wrong. Trust us. Always write everything down.

Read and Copy Carefully

You can do all the calculations right and still get a question wrong. How? What if you solve for x but the question was "What is the value of $x + 3$?" Ugh. Always reread the question. Take your time and don't be careless. The question will stay on the screen; it's not going anywhere.

Or, how about this? The radius of the circle is 6, but when you copied the picture onto your scratch paper, you accidentally made it 5. Ugh! Many of the mistakes you make at first might stem from copying information down incorrectly. Learn from your mistakes! You need to be extra careful when copying down information.

Accuracy Versus Speed

You don't get points for speed; the only thing that matters is accuracy. Take some time to work through each problem carefully (as long as you leave some time at the end of the section to fill out the rest of it). If you're making careless errors, you won't even realize you're getting questions wrong. Get into the habit of double-checking all of your answers before you choose them. However, don't get too bogged down on a question. When you get stuck, mark the question, walk away, and return after you've answered a few other questions.

At the Testing Center

You'll be asked for two forms of identification; one must be a photo ID. Then, an employee will take a digital photograph of you before taking you to the computer station where you will take the test. You get a desk, a computer, a keyboard, a mouse, about six pieces of scratch paper, and two pencils. Before the test begins, make sure your desk is sturdy and you have enough light, and don't be afraid to speak up if you want to move.

If there are other people in the room, they might not be taking the GRE CAT. They could be taking a nursing test, or a licensing exam for architects. And they will not necessarily have started their exams at the same time. The testing center employee will get you set up at your computer, but from then on, the computer itself will act as your proctor. It'll tell you how much time you have left in a section, when time is up, and when to move on to the next section.

The test center employees will be available because they will be monitoring the testing room for security purposes with closed-circuit television. But don't worry, you won't even notice. If you have a question, or need to request more scratch paper during the test, try to do so between the timed sections.

Let It Go

When you begin a new section, focus on that section and put the last one behind you. Don't think about that pesky antonym from an earlier section while a geometry question is on your screen. You can't go back, and besides, your impression of how you did on a section is probably much worse than reality. Remember, the test adapts so that it is hard for everyone.

This Is the End

When you're done with the test, the computer will ask you twice if you want this test to count. If you say "no," the computer will not record your score, no schools will ever see it, and neither will you. You can't look at your score and then decide whether you want to keep it or not. And you can't change your mind later. If you say you want the test to count, the computer will give you your Verbal and Math scores right there on the screen. A few weeks later, you'll receive your verified score in the mail. You can't change your mind and cancel it.

TEST DAY CHECKLIST

Dress in layers so that you'll be comfortable regardless of whether the room is cool or warm.

Be sure to have breakfast, or lunch, depending on the time your test is scheduled (but don't eat anything, you know, "weird"). And go easy on the liquids and caffeine.

Do a few GRE practice problems to warm up your brain. Don't try to tackle difficult new questions, but review a few questions that you've done before to help you review the problem-solving strategies for each section of the GRE. This will also help you put your "game-face" on and get you into test mode.

Make sure to bring two forms of identification (one with a recent photograph) to the test center. Acceptable forms of identification include driver's licenses, photo-bearing employee ID cards, and valid passports.

If you registered by mail, you must also bring the authorization voucher sent to you by ETS.

The Week of the Test

A week before the test is not the time for any major life changes. This is not the week to quit smoking, start smoking, quit drinking coffee, start drinking coffee, start a relationship, end a relationship, or quit a job. Business as usual, okay? If you're taking the new test between August and October 2011, you won't see your score until November 15, 2011.

PART II

TEN STEPS TO SCORING HIGHER ON THE GRE

USE SCRATCH PAPER FOR VERBAL QUESTIONS

USE SCRATCH PAPER FOR VERBAL QUESTIONS

Most people answer verbal questions in their heads. Heck, most people will answer half the math questions in their heads as well, which is suicide if you ask us! When you answer a verbal question in your head, you are really doing two things at once. The first is evaluating each answer choice, one by one, and the second is keeping track of which answer choices are in or out. A recent study of multitasking (trying to do multiple things at the same time) showed that it can't be done well. The brain is simply not equipped to do too many things correctly at once. What most people call multitasking is really schizophrenically jumping back and forth between multiple tasks. The study also showed that people who attempt to multitask inevitably end up doing both tasks worse. Really. Those super efficient multi-taskers we always hear about are a myth. People who try to multitask make more mistakes because they are constantly distracting their brains from the task at hand. Doing verbal questions in your head is multitasking. It leads to careless and avoidable mistakes, mistakes that could be catastrophic to your score.

The solution is to engage your hand. This means using scratch paper. Yes, scratch paper is every bit as important on the verbal side of the test as it is on the math side of the test. If your hand is not moving, you are stuck thinking. Thinking does not get you any closer to the answer. You should be doing, not thinking, while taking the GRE.

Here is what verbal scratch paper looks like on the GRE:

Scratch paper allows you to park your thinking on the page. On the verbal side of the test, there will always be words or answers you don't know. Looking for the right answer, therefore, will work only part of the time. Fortunately the majority of the verbal section is multiple-choice. They've actually given you the answers, and one of those answers is correct. If you can't identify the right answer, you can always identify some wrong ones. You're probably doing this already; you're just not capturing the results on the page.

Once you start parking that thinking on the page, however, a few good things happen. The first is that you avoid redundant work. Once you eliminate an answer choice, it's gone. You need never look at it again. Next, you save time because you aren't going back over ground you've already covered. And the last benefit is that you save yourself lots of mental effort. It's hard keeping track of all of those decisions in your head. During a four-hour test, your brain is going to get tired. Saving mental effort makes a difference.

Use these symbols on your scratch paper to capture your progress:

✔   This means you know the answer choice, and it looks right. It doesn't mean that you are done. You must always check every answer choice, but it does mean that you've got one that looks good. Give it a check and move on to the next one.

~   In some ways, this one is the most important because you're going to use it all the time. On your first pass through the answer choices, it's important to keep moving. Don't get hung up on a single answer choice. When you're not sure about an answer choice, the first thing that everyone does is stop and think. On the GRE we want to be doing, not thinking. You should be looking for wrong answers not right ones. Rather than spending time thinking about a single answer choice, give it the "maybe" and move on. It is entirely possible that the other four answer choices are wrong, or that you come across one that is clearly right. In either case, time spent agonizing over an answer choice about which you're not sure is time wasted. *Keep your hand moving.*

$\cancel{A}$ We love this one. When you know something is wrong, get rid of it. You never want to spend time on that answer choice ever again. Even if you have to guess, you want to guess from as few answer choices as possible. There are about four times the number of wrong answers on the GRE as there are right ones. The wrong ones are much, much easier to find. Identify them and eliminate them. Keep track with your hand.

?   If you don't know a word, you can't eliminate it. Be honest with yourself. If you don't like the word, you don't have to pick it, but you can't eliminate it. But you should not waste a lot of time on it. Give it a question mark and move on to the next answer choice.

In all cases, the place to invest your time is in the question stem and in coming up with your own answer choice. The answer choices are designed to tempt and to mislead you. By the time you get to the answer choices, your first pass through should be quick—10 or 15 seconds, tops. Either you know the word or answer choice and it works, you know it and it doesn't work, or you don't know it. Anything else gets the "maybe." Making this evaluation takes very little time.

With your evaluations parked on the page, your scratch paper can often answer the question for you. Consider the these five common scenarios:

1. $\cancel{A}$, $\cancel{B}$, $\cancel{C}$, $\sim$, $\checkmark$ If you have an answer choice and it works, go with it. Look at this scratch paper. Your decision is made.

2. $\cancel{A}$, $\cancel{B}$, $\cancel{C}$, ?, $\cancel{D}$ What more do you need to know? You have four wrong answers and one you don't know. If the other four are wrong, they're wrong. You have no choice. There is only one possible answer choice that it could be.

3. $\cancel{A}$, $\sim$, $\cancel{C}$, $\sim$, E   If you need to spend more time on an answer choice, you always can, but don't do it until you have to. In this case, you're down to two. Do what you can to inform your guess, but don't go crazy. Pick one and move on or skip and come back.

4. A̶, B̶, C̶, D̶, E̶ You've eliminated all five. Something's gone wrong. Most likely, you've misread something in the question or something in the answer choices. You'll never see your mistake unless you distract your brain. Mark the question, walk away, and come back after you've done a few others.

5. A̶, ?, C̶, ?, E You're down to two. You don't know the words. You've eliminated all that you can. Spend no more time. Pick an answer and move on.

Here are a few examples:

Which of the following is not the capital of a county in Europe?
○ Istanbul
○ Luxembourg
○ Monaco
○ Vaduz
○ Walletta

Engage the hand and work out the problem on your scratch paper. Each question should take less than 25 seconds.

Now try this one:

Which of the following was not one of the original Seven Wonders of the Ancient World?
○ The Colossus of Rhodes
○ The Great Pyramid of Giza
○ The Great Wall of China
○ The Hanging Gardens of Babylon
○ The Lighthouse at Alexandria

Verbal scratch paper is a habit. Start practicing it now and force yourself to use it. The more you use it, the more it will ease your decision making. Eventually, you won't be able to do it any other way. This is the goal. It's hard work at first, but good techniques should become instinctual, physical, and automatic.

SLOW DOWN
FOR READING
COMPREHENSION

SLOW DOWN FOR READING COMPREHENSION

Reading Comprehension is an open-book test. The answers are in the passage. With unlimited time, in theory, you should never get a reading comprehension question wrong. There are three ways you can give yourself more time on reading comprehension.

- The first is to get so good at text completions and sentence equivalence that you have plenty of time left over for reading comp, where time equals points.
- The second way to pick up time is to pick your battles. Take on fewer passages, do fewer questions, but get more right. Rushing through reading comp guarantees wrong answers. Slow down and make sure that the time you spend yields points.
- The last way to give yourself more time on reading comp is to be smart about where you spend your time. There is a lot of information in the passages, but you will be tested on only a tiny portion of that information. A smart and efficient strategy for working with the passages will pay dividends in the form of more time and less stress.

There are three basic components of reading comprehension:

The Passages

ETS does not write the passages. They license the rights to a few books at a time and then mine those books for reading comp passages, text completion passages, and sentence equivalence sentences. Because of this, it is not uncommon to see the same subjects pop up more than once on a given test. Most authors strive for clarity. Too much clarity, however, is a problem if you need to write a difficult test. So ETS will manipulate the passages to make them harder to work with. To do this, they start with a 1,200-word passage (passages could range in length from 250 words to 1,000 words) and then will shrink it down to about 1,000 words for a long passage. To shrink it down, they get rid of explanations, definitions, clear subject-verb-object sentences, and anything else that makes good, clear writing good and clear. They keep in extraneous facts you will never need to know, long twisting sentences with lots changes in direction (it's not at all uncommon for the entire first paragraph of a passage to be one long sentence), poorly defined technical terms, and anything else that will make it hard to absorb all of the information in a given passage after a single reading. The passages are designed to be dense and difficult to read.

The Questions

You'll notice that most of the questions aren't really questions at all. They're really incomplete sentences. Before you even start looking for an answer, you have to find the question in the question!

The Answer Choices

There are a number of different games that ETS loves to play with the answer choices. First they will give you an answer choice that is clearly supported by the passage but does not answer the question and so is wrong. Or, they will give you an answer choice that does answer the question, but they'll twist it just slightly so that it is wrong. Or they will give you an answer that perfectly answers the question but that isn't supported by information in the passage and is therefore wrong. The answer choices are carefully designed to mislead. Unless you have a crystal clear idea of what you are looking for, some of the wrong answer choices can be mighty tempting.

> The number one golden rule of reading comprehension is this: If you cannot put your finger on a word, phrase, or sentence in the passage that proves your answer choice, you cannot pick it.

For every single question, you must always go back to the passage and find proof. Always. No exceptions. The minute you stop reading, you start forgetting, and no one can remember all of the information in these passages anyway. ETS will exploit your memory of the passage with tempting but wrong answer choices. When you answer a question from memory, you make their job even easier.

As long as you have to go back to the passage for proof for every question anyway, the obvious question, then, is how much of the passage should you read in the first place?

This depends upon four criteria:

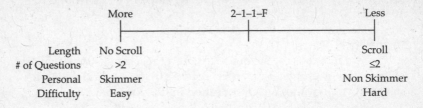

	More	2–1–1–F	Less
Length	No Scroll		Scroll
# of Questions	>2		≤2
Personal	Skimmer		Non Skimmer
Difficulty	Easy		Hard

> You can always read more of a passage if you have to, but you never want to read more than you have to.

To start a passage, you need to know three things: the main idea, the structure, and the tone. Let's say a passage is about a problem scientists are trying to solve. To get started, all you need to know is that there is a question, scientists are trying to answer it, but they haven't yet. The rest is just details. You may eventually need to know these details or you may not, but you can look for them on a question-by-question basis, as needed.

A good place to start reading for the main idea without getting bogged down in the details is 2-1-1-F. This means that you read the first two sentences of a passage, the first sentence of each additional paragraph, and the final sentence of the passage. Generally, this will be sufficient to give you the main idea of the passage. If it is not, no problem; just read a bit more. *Remember: You are going to go back to the passage to find proof for every problem, no matter what, anyway.* You do not need comprehensive knowledge of the whole passage at this point.

Here's a sample passage with 2-1-1-F highlighted:

> It is well known that termites are blind, but little has been discovered about the other sense organs of these insects or their reactions to various stimuli. Body odors, as well as odors related to sex and to colony, certainly play a part in the activities of the termite colony. When specimens of eastern subterranean termites are placed in a jar containing a colony of rotten wood termites from the Pacific Coast, the host termites recognize these foreign insects by differences in odor and eventually kill the invaders. The progress of the chase and kill is very slow, and the

larger host termites appear awkward in their efforts to bite and kill their smaller but quicker-moving cousins. Finally, more or less by sheer numbers and by accident, they corner and exterminate the enemy.

Eastern dealated (wingless) termites that manage to survive in the rotten wood termite colony for more than a week, however, are no longer molested. This is noteworthy, because eastern termites of this variety had previously been pursued and killed. Fresh eastern wingless specimens placed in the colony alongside the week-old visitors are immediately attacked, thus indicating that the rotten wood termites have in no way lost their capacity for belligerence.

What else besides odor helps termites interpret the world around them? The insects have sense or "chorodontal" organs located on the antennae, on the bristles, on the base of the mandibles, and on the legs. These organs apparently enable termites to receive vibrations sent through the air, or, more precisely, aid in the reception of stimuli sent through the nest material or through air pockets within the nest material. When alarmed, soldier termites exhibit synchronous, convulsive movements that appear to be a method of communication adapted to the chorodontal organ system, although no sound that is audible to man is produced by these movements. Termite soldiers also strike their heads against wood and other nest materials, producing noises that, after passing through the sounding board formed by the nest material, become rustling and crackling sounds plainly audible to man's duller and possibly differently attuned perceptions. In fact, soldiers of one termite species, found in the arid regions of California, strike their heads against the dry, dead flower stalks of Spanish bayonets and agave plants with such force that the sound produced can be heard several feet away. Other types of soldier termites found in the tropics make audible clicking noises with their jaws.

There is a clear correlation between the functioning of the chorodontal system and termite settlement patterns. Seldom are termites found infesting railroad ties over which there is frequent heavy traffic, or on the woodwork of mill or factory buildings where heavy machinery in motion would cause vibrations. Small-scale tests with a radio speaker and vibrator yielded interesting results when termites were placed in the speaker and exposed to various frequency vibrations. When the vibrations ranged from 50–100 per second, the termites were thrown about; at vibrations of 100–500, termites set their feet and mandibles and held on with all their power; at 2,000–5,000 vibrations per second, the termites crawled about undisturbed.

What's the passage about?
Termites and how they perceive the world (they're blind).
Do we know the answer?
No. But we have some clues. Something about order, the chorodontal system, and vibrations.
Does the author take a position?
Nope, purely a description of a scientific exploration.

How long did it take you to read those six sentences? Less than a minute, right? You now know the main idea of the passage, roughly what each paragraph is about, and the tone. Best of all, you haven't spent a lot of time, and you haven't been distracted by lots of useless and confusing details.

The Questions

When it comes to answering specific questions, there is a basic five step process:

Step 1. **Read the question**—You can answer questions in any order you like. Some questions, like a main idea question, you are already equipped to answer. Other questions may ask you to prove four or five answer choices, and these you might want to save until you've spent more time with the passage.

Step 2. **Make the question into a question**—In order to find an answer, you must have a question. Most questions ask you either "what was stated in the passage" or "why was it said?" The easiest way to make the question into a question, therefore, is to simply start with a question word. Most of the time, "what" or "why" will do the trick. Note: In this step you are also engaging in the question in a qualitative way. This is important because your brain is going to get tired, and when it does, it is all too easy to skim a question and have no idea what it's really asking.

Step 3. **Find proof**—Always go back to the passage and find proof. If they highlight a portion of the passage, start reading four or five lines before the highlighted section and read until four or five lines after. You always want to look at things in context. If they don't highlight the text, use a lead word (any word that will be easy to skim for in the passage: names, dates, technical terms, anything with a capital letter—all make good lead words), and then read five lines up and five lines down.

Step 4. **Answer the question in your own words**—Remember that the answer choices are designed to tempt and mislead you. They are very good at it. If you don't have a clear sense of what you're looking for, they'll serve up some mighty tempting, but wrong, answer choices. If you do know what you're looking for, wrong answers will look wrong and right ones will look right.

Before we get to step five, let's look at a few questions:
The author's primary concern in the passage is to

1. **Read the question:** Done

2. **What is this question asking?** What is the main idea of the passage: Termites and how they perceive the world (they're blind).

3. **Find proof:** Go back to 2-1-1-F. Do we need more? Nope.

4. **Answer the question in your own words:** Investigate ways the termite perceives the world if it's not through the eyes.

Now you're equipped to handle the answer choices (answer choices to follow).

According to the passage, a termite's jaw can be important in all of the following EXCEPT

1. **Read the question:** Done. This question asks us to chase down five pieces of information about the termite's jaw. That's a lot of work. We might want to leave this one for the end.

It can be inferred from the passage that dealated eastern termites that have survived a week in a rotten wood termite colony are no longer attacked because they

1. **Read the question:** Done

2. **Make the question into a question:** Why are "dealated termites" that survive a week, no longer attacked?

3. **Find proof:** "Dealated termites" will make a good lead word. Skim the passage until you find it, and then read five lines up and five lines down.

4. **Answer the question in your own words:** You've got to read quite a bit of the first paragraph, and most of the second paragraph to figure this one out. (Good thing we didn't waste time reading all of this on the first pass then we'd end up reading it twice.) It seems that after a week, the eastern termites no longer smell bad.

The Answer Choices:

Step 5. Use Process of Elimination—Do not look for right answers. You will always be able to find a reason why an answer could be right. Look for the wrong ones. If you find a reason why an answer is wrong, you can eliminate it. If you can't find a reason it's wrong, that's a good sign that it's right. Always stick to things that you can objectively prove with the passage.

There are some common reasons answer choices are wrong:

Extremes—Beware of extreme language. Extreme language is too easy to argue with. ETS prefers to play it safe, so they phrase correct answers in nice, wishy-washy language that is difficult to argue with.

Scope—If it's not in the passage, you can't pick. Watch out for answer choices that include things never mentioned in the passage. On main idea questions, watch out for answer choices that are too specific.

Common Sense—Not all answer choices make sense. Just because it's on the test, doesn't mean that you can't laugh at it—and eliminate it.

Let's try a few out, but first get your scratch paper out and get ready to start marking up answer choices.

The author's primary concern in the passage is to

- ⬭ show how little is known of certain organ systems in insects
- ⬭ describe the termite's method of overcoming blindness
- ⬭ provide an overview of some termite sensory organs
- ⬭ relate the termite's sensory perceptions to man's
- ⬭ describe the termite's aggressive behavior

What does the question ask? What is the main idea of the passage: Investigate ways the termite perceives the world if it's not through the eyes.

Answer: Investigate ways the termite perceives the world if it's not through the eyes.

(A) If the passage is about termites, then the answer to a main idea question had better mention termites. Cross off (A).

(B) Hmmm. Possibly, but if the termites don't know they're blind, they're not overcoming anything. Give it the "maybe."

(C) This is possible. Give it a check.

(D) Whoa! Even if this was mentioned, it's certainly not the main idea. Cross off (D).

(E) Whoa again! Might be true, but what about odor, and the choronodtal system, and everything else? Get rid of it.

Now check your scratch paper. You've got a "maybe" and a "check." If you've got one that works, go with it. You're done.

It can be inferred from the passage that dealated eastern termites that have survived a week in a rotten wood termite colony are no longer attacked because they

○ have come to resemble the rotten wood termites in most ways

○ no longer have an odor provocative to the rotten wood termites

○ no longer pose a threat to the host colony

○ have learned to resonate at the same frequency as the host group

○ have changed the pattern in which they use their mandibles

What does the question ask? Why are "dealated termites" that survive a week, no longer attacked?

What's the answer in your own words? Because after a week the
eastern termites no longer smell bad.

(A) This is a little extreme. They change shape? Change size? Got a
hair cut? Cross it off.

(B) Talks about smell. Give it a check.

(C) Do we know this? Can we prove it? They might still be a threat.
Cross it off.

(D) Resonate, huh? Cross it off.

(E) Mandibles, huh? Cross it off.

The answer is (B).

> According to the passage, a termite's
> jaw can be important in all of the fol-
> lowing EXCEPT
> ○ aggression against intruders of
>   other termite species
> ○ the reception of vibrations sent by
>   other termites
> ○ stabilization of the insect against
>   physical disturbances
> ○ the production of sound made by
>   striking wood or plants
> ○ sounding an alert to notify other
>   termites of danger

What does the question ask? What does the passage tell us about
termite jaws?

What to skim for? Jaws.

What's the answer in your own words? Hmm. This is an EXCEPT/
LEAST/NOT question. For these you really have to answer four questions but get credit for only one. It's best to treat these like a true/
false question. First look at everything the passage says about jaws:
Termites bite and kill other termites, they can receive vibrations on
their mandibles (another word for jaws), they can make clicking
noises, and they use their jaws to hang on to things that are moving.

Let's check the answer choices:

   (A)   True. Bottom of the first paragraph.

   (B)   True. Top of the third paragraph.

   (C)   True. Last sentence of the passage.

   (D)   Not sure. Give this a question mark.

   (E)   True. They make a clicking sound.

One of these things is not like the other. The answer is (D).

Don't be afraid of the "maybe." If you're not sure about an answer choice, don't get hung up on it; just give it the "maybe" and move on to the next one. If you are stuck on a problem, walk away. Do a few other questions and then return to the one that was giving you trouble. What you learn when answering one question often turns out to be helpful on another. The correct answer to any problem will always support or parallel the main idea of the passage. If you find yourself down to two, and you are convinced that both answer choices are right, you are misreading something. Walk away and come back after a few questions. When you return, try paraphrasing the answer choices as well.

Special Format Questions

There are three types of questions you might see with Reading Comprehension:

   1.   Multiple Choice

   2.   Select All That Apply

   3.   Select In Passage

1. **Multiple Choice**—These are the standard, five-choice, multiple-choice questions we have been doing. There is only one correct answer choice and four wrong ones.

2. **Select All That Apply**—These are a variation of the old Roman numeral questions. Remember the ones that gave you three statements marked I, II, and III, and the answer choices that say, "I only," "I and II only," "I, II, and III"? These are the same, but without the answer choices. They will give you three statements, with a box next to each. You have to select all that apply. The process is the same. Find lead words and look for proof.

3. **Select In Passage**—In this case, ETS will ask you to select a sentence in the passage that makes a particular point, or raises a question, or provides proof, or some other function. These questions will appear primarily on short passages. If one appears on a longer passage, they will limit the scope to a particular paragraph. Again, the same rules apply. Pick a lead word. Put the question into your own words, and use Process of Elimination. To answer one of these, you will literally click on a particular sentence in the passage or paragraph.

Three things to keep in mind when working on Reading Comprehension:

1. You need only general knowledge of the passage to get started. Don't get bogged down in the details.

2. Always answer the question in your own words before you look at the answer choices.

3. Look for reasons why an answer choice is wrong, not reasons why it is right. Park that thinking on your scratch paper. If your hand is not moving, you're stuck. Move on.

Above all: Find proof in the passage for every answer you select. If there's no proof, it's not the right answer.

COVER UP THE ANSWERS FOR SENTENCE EQUIVALENCE

COVER UP THE ANSWERS FOR SENTENCE EQUIVALENCE

Here are the directions for sentence equivalence: Select the two answer choices that, when used to complete the sentence, fit the meaning of the sentence as a whole and produce completed sentences that are alike in meaning.

In other words, figure out the story being told and pick the two words in the answer choices that complete the story in the same way. These are, in effect, sentence-completion questions, but you are picking two words rather than one for the same blank.

The other part of sentence equivalence is the answer choices. They will always fit grammatically into the sentence and quite a few of them will make a degree of sense. They represent ETS's suggestions for what to put in the blank. We don't like their suggestions, we don't trust their suggestions, and we don't want their suggestions. The answer choices have been carefully selected and then tested on thousands of students for the sole purpose of messing with your head. The first step on sentence equivalence is always to cover up the answer choices. Literally. Put your hand on the screen and don't let them in.

Back to the sentence; think of this as a mini reading comprehension passage. Before you do anything, find the main idea. Who is the passage talking about? What are we told about this person or thing? Once you have the story firmly in mind, come up with your own word for the blank, and eliminate the answer choices that don't match.

Let's try one:

> Wilson worked _____ on his first novel, cloistering himself in his study for days on end without food or sleep.
>
> ☐ carelessly
>
> ☐ assiduously
>
> ☐ creatively
>
> ☐ tirelessly
>
> ☐ intermittently
>
> ☐ voluntarily

Step 1—Cover the answer choices.

Step 2—Find the story. Who is our main character? Wilson. What are we told about Wilson? He's working on his first novel and has locked himself in his study for a long time without food or sleep. The dude is working hard. The blank, in fact, describes how Wilson is working.

Step 3—Come up with your own word for the blank. Hard? Dedicated? Unceasing?

Step 4—Use Process Of Elimination (POE). Use your word to eliminate answer choices. Of each answer choice, ask yourself, "Does this word mean the same thing as or similar to _____ (my word)?" If the answer is no, get rid of it. If the answer is "I'm not sure," give it the maybe and move on. If the answer is yes, give it the check. All of this work takes place on your scratch paper.

(A) Does *carelessly* mean the same thing as or similar to *hard, dedicated,* or *unceasing*? No. Cross off choice (A).

(B) Does *assiduously* mean the same thing as or similar to *hard, dedicated,* or *unceasing*? Not sure? Give it the question mark and leave it in.

(C) Does *creatively* mean the same thing as or similar to *hard, dedicated,* or *unceasing*? No. Could Wilson, the first-time novelist, be working creatively? Sure, but it's not what we're looking for. Cross off choice (C).

(D) Does *tirelessly* mean the same thing as or similar to *hard, dedicated,* or *unceasing*? Sure does. Give it a check.

(E) Does *intermittently* mean the same thing as or similar to *hard, dedicated,* or *unceasing*? Nope. Cross off choice (E).

(F) Does *voluntarily* mean the same thing as or similar to *hard, dedicated,* or *unceasing*? Nope. Cross off choice (F).

Now look at your scratch paper. You have four that are no, a yes, and a question mark. You're done. Whatever *assiduously* means, it must be similar to *hard, dedicated,* or *unceasing*. The correct answers are *tirelessly* and *assiduously*.

Finding the Clue

How did you know to put *hard, dedicated,* or *unceasing* in the blank? The sentence says, "cloistering himself in his study for days on end without food or sleep." What else could it be? That part of the sentence is what we call a clue. Every sentence will have one. Every sentence must have one because it's the part of the sentence that makes one answer right and another one wrong. The clue is like an arrow that points only to right answers. Finding the clue will help to come up with your own word for the blank and will help to eliminate wrong answers. You try:

Drill 1

In each of the following sentences, find the clue and underline it. Then, write down your own word for the blank. It doesn't matter if your guesses are awkward or wordy. All you need to do is express the right idea.

1. Despite the apparent _____ of the demands, the negotiations dragged on for over a year.

2. Most students found Dr. Schwartz's lecture on art excessively detailed and academic; some thought his display of _____ exasperating.

Drill 2

Now look at the same questions again, this time with the answer choices provided. Use your words above to eliminate answer choices (answers can be found at the end of the chapter):

1. Despite the apparent _____ of the demands, the negotiations dragged on for over a year.
   - hastiness
   - intolerance
   - publicity
   - modesty
   - desirability
   - triviality

2. Most students found Dr. Schwartz's lecture on art excessively detailed and academic; some thought his display of _____ exasperating.

○ pedantry
○ fundamentals
○ logic
○ aesthetics
○ erudition
○ literalism

Trigger Words

Imagine a conversation that begins, "That's Frank. He won the lottery and now _____." Something good is going to go into that blank. Frank could be a millionaire, could be living on his own island, or could be a great collector of rare jeweled belt buckles. Whatever it is, this story is going to end happily.

Now consider this story: "That's Frank. He won the lottery but now _____." This story is going to end badly. Frank could be tied up in court for tax evasion, could be pan handling on the corner, or could be in a mental institution.

The only difference between these two stories is the words *but* and *and*. These are trigger words.

They provide important structural indicators of the meaning of the sentence, and are often the key to figuring out what words have to mean to fill in the blanks in a sentence completion. Here are some of the most important sentence completion trigger words and punctuation:

but	in contrast
although (though, even though)	unfortunately
unless	heretofore
rather	thus
yet	and
despite	therefore
while	similarly
however	; *or* :

Paying attention to trigger words is crucial to understanding the meaning of the sentence, thereby helping you to speak for yourself. The words from *but* to *heretofore* are "change direction" trigger words, indicating that the two parts of the sentence diverge in meaning. The above words, from *thus* to the colon (:) and semi-colon (;), are "some direction" triggers, indicating that the two parts of the above sentence agree. For example, if your sentence said "Judy was a fair and _____ judge," the placement of the "and" would tell you that the word in the blank would have to be similar to "fair." You could even use the word "fair" as your fill-in-the-blank word.

What if your sentence said, "Judy was a fair but _____ judge"? The placement of the "but" would tell you that the word in the blank would have to be somewhat opposite of "fair," something like "tough."

Let's try this one (we're taking the answer choices away again, for now):

> Although originally created for _____
> use, the colorful, stamped tin kitchen
> boxes of the early twentieth century
> are now prized primarily for their orna-
> mental qualities.

What's the clue in the sentence that tells us why the boxes were originally created? Well, we know that they "are now prized primarily for their ornamental qualities." Does this mean that they were originally created for "ornamental" use? No. The trigger word "although" indicates that the word for the blank will mean the opposite of "ornamental." How about "useful"? It may sound strange to say "useful use," but don't worry about how your words sound—it's what they mean that's important.

Now, here are the answer choices:

- ○ utilitarian
- ○ traditional
- ○ practical
- ○ occasional
- ○ annual
- ○ commercial

(A) Does "utilitarian" mean useful? Yes, give it a check on your scratch paper.

(B) Does "traditional" mean useful? No. Cross it off on your scratch paper.

(C) Does "practical" mean useful? Yes, give it a check mark.

(D) Does "occasional" mean useful? Nope. Get rid of it.

(E) Does "annual" mean useful? Nope, cross it off.

(F) Does "commercial" mean useful? No. Cross it off.

The answers are (A) and (C)]

Positive/Negative

In some cases, you may think of several words that could go in the blanks. Or, you might not be able to think of any. Rather than spend a lot of time trying to find the "perfect" word, just ask yourself whether the missing word will be a positive word or a negative word. Then, write a + or a – symbol on your scratch paper and take it from there. Here's an example (again, without answer choices, for now):

> Trembling with anger, the belligerent colonel ordered his men to _____ the civilians.

Use those clues. We know the colonel is "trembling with anger," and that he's "belligerent" (which means war-like). Is the missing word a "good" word or a "bad" word? It's a "bad" word. The colonel is clearly going to do something nasty to the civilians. Now we can go to the answer choices and eliminate any choices that are positive and therefore couldn't be correct:

○ congratulate
○ promote
○ reward
○ attack
○ worship
○ torment

Choices A, B, C, and E are all positive words; therefore, they can all be eliminated. The only negative words among the choices are (D and (F), the best answers. Positive/negative won't work for every question, but sometimes it can get you out of a jam.

When it comes to Text Completions, remember these three things:

1. **Invest your time in the sentence.** Stick with the sentence until you find the story. You cannot go to the answer choices until that story is crystal clear.

2. **Use your word as your filter.** Come up with your own word for the blank and use it to eliminate answer choices. You should be actively identifying and eliminating wrong answers. Keep your hand moving on your scratch paper. Processing the answer choices should take no more than 20 seconds. Note: If an answer choice has no synonym among the other answer choices, it's unlikely to be correct.

3. **Mark and come back.** If a sentence isn't making sense, or none of the answer choices look right, walk away. Don't keep forcing the sentence. You may have read something wrong. Go do a few other questions to distract your brain and then take a second look at it.

FILL IN THE BLANKS ON TEXT COMPLETION

FILL IN THE BLANKS ON TEXT COMPLETION

Text Completions occupy a middle ground between sentence equivalence and reading comprehension. You will be given a small passage—one to five sentences—with one, two, or three blanks. If the passage has one blank, you will have five answer choices. If it has two or three blanks, you will be given three answer choices per blank. You have to independently fill in each blank to get credit for the question.

The overall approach is the same. Ignore the answer choices. Find the story being told (there will always be a story), and come up with your own words for the blanks. Here's what a three-blank text completion will look like:

Sample Question

Directions: For each blank, select one entry from the corresponding column of choices. Fill all blanks in the way that best completes the text.

Question 12 of 20

The image of the architect as the lonely artist drawing three dimensional forms is ___(i)___ the public's understanding of the architect's role. As a result, buildings are viewed as the singular creations of an artistic vision with the artist ___(ii)___ the architect. Certainly architects should take much of the credit for the form of a unique building, but the final product is hardly a ___(iii)___. The architect relies heavily upon façade consultants, engineers, and skilled builders, while the form of the building may depend, in addition, upon zoning regulations, cost, and market demands.

Blank (i)	Blank (ii)	Blank (iii)
at odds with	tangentially related to	virtuoso performance
central to	but an after-thought to	collaborative effort
irrelevant to	justifiably embodied by	physical triumph

Step 1—Find the story. In this case, the story is about the public perception of the role of the architect versus the actual role of the architect.

Step 2—Prep your scratch paper. As opposed to columns of A's, B's, C's, D's, E's, and F's, text completion scratch paper will look like this:

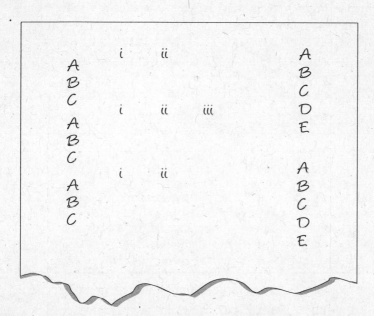

Step 3—Pick a blank. Some blanks will be easier to fill in than others. In general, blanks have two roles. They test either vocabulary or comprehension. A blank testing vocabulary may be easy to fill in with your own words, but then the answer choices may consist of difficult vocabulary words. A blank testing comprehension may depend upon what you put in another blank, or it may contain multiple words, including a few trigger words and prepositions. Start with whichever blank seems the easiest. In this case the last blank may be the easiest.

Step 4—Speak for yourself. The sentence contains the trigger word "but." Trigger words are always significant. Sensitize yourself to trigger words. They always come into play. The passage says that the architect should get lots of credit for a building, BUT...it is clear that other people should get some credit too. Come up with your own words for the blanks. The final product is clearly not "the architects alone."

Step 5—Use POE. There are three choices. "Virtuoso performance" sounds like "the architects alone." Keep it in. "Collaborative effort" is the opposite of what we're looking for. Get rid of it. "Physical triumph" introduces a new concept to the sentence. That automatically knocks it out. A correct answer choice will always be supported by proof in the passage. An answer choice that adds something new to the sentence (physicality, in this case) is automatically wrong. At this point, the story in the sentence is quite clear, and your scratch paper should look like this:

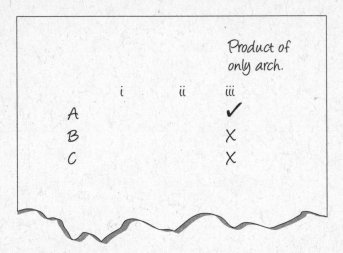

Step 6—Rinse and Repeat.

For the first blank, the way buildings are viewed should be similar to the way architects are viewed. Even if you can't come up with a word for the first blank, you at least know that you need something that keeps the sentence going in the same direction. Of the three choices, "at odds with" clearly changes the direction, so get rid of it. "Irrelevant to" is neutral at best, so get rid of it. "Central to" is the only answer choice in the same direction. Give it a check.

For the second blank, thinking in terms of direction will work well again. In this story, what is the relationship between the "artist" and the "architect"? The two seem to serve the same function. We need an answer choice that indicates equivalence. "Justifiably embodied by" is the closest thing in the answer choices to an equal sign.

Here's what your scratch paper should look like:

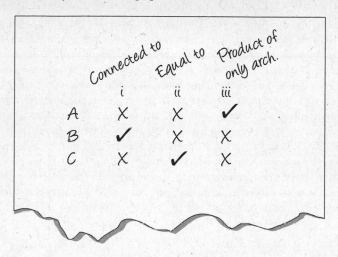

That may seem like a long process, but it's really just a way of thinking. Find the story. Play close attention to trigger words. Come up with words for the blank or establish direction. Keep the hand moving and eliminate.

Let's try one more.

Despite hundreds of _____(i)_____ attempts to produce a working light bulb, Edison eventually triumphed, his _____(ii)_____ contributing to his ultimate success.

Blank (i)	Blank (ii)
felicitous	grandiloquence
stymied	indifference
auspicious	tenacity

Who's the main character and what's the story being told? The sentence is about Edison and his attempts to make a working light bulb. There are two key words in this sentence, "despite" and "eventually." "Despite" tells us that the sentence has to change direction and "eventually" tells us that it took a long time. The end of the sentence describes his "ultimate success," so the beginning must contain some failure. Put "failed" in for the first blank and eliminate. Felicitous (think felicity) and auspicious are both positive words, so cross them off. Stymied stays in. We also know that the process took a long time, so Edison must have been the kind of guy that doesn't give up. Let's put "stick with it-ness" in for the second blank. You don't have to put a perfect ETS word in the blank. Anything that captures the meaning or idea will do. Grandiloquence has to do with the way you talk, which is not what we're looking for, so cross it off. Indifference does not mean stubbornness, so get rid of it. We're down to one, so we're done.

Here are a few key concepts to keep in mind:

1. **Scratch Paper**—Using scratch paper favors an efficient "maybe or gone," two-pass approach through the answer choices. With text completion there are effectively 6-9 answer choices rather than 5. Scratch paper is crucial.

2. **Clues**—In a regular sent camp question, if the word in the blank is a noun, some other part of the sentence will describe the noun. If it is a verb, there will be some other part of the sentence describing the subject or object of that verb. If it is an adjective. there will invariably be some other part of the sentence describing the noun that the adjective is modifying. This is the essence of what makes a clue a clue. The same concept holds true here but on a slightly larger scale. Whatever information is missing in one sentence must be present in another one. It is the only way for there to be an identifiably correct answer. If the concept of the clue feels too abstract, think of it as the story being told. Every sentence will tell a story. Who is the main character, what is the main character doing and what are you told about the main character? If you don't have the

story firmly in focus, you're in trouble. Just like text completion, the answer choices represent ETS's suggestions for what to put in the blank. In fact. the answer choices have been painstakingly selected and tested with the sole purpose of messing with your head. Unless you can physically put your finger on a clue or key sentence. you are at the mercy of ETS and the answer choices.

3. **Directional Versus Vocabulary**—It is always preferable, or more exact, to come up with your own words for the blank. While sometimes necessary or even effective, simply deciding whether a blank calls for a good word or bad word can be a crutch for the lazy. With text completion, however, the answer choices may be all about whether the text will keep the sentence moving in the same direction or the opposite direction. In other words, it is often the trigger words or phrases that you are being asked to supply. With only three answer choices, simply identifying either the necessary direction or need for a positive or negative word may take care of all of the elimination you need to get it down to one answer choice.

Know Your Math Vocabulary

IT'S A READING TEST

ETS says that the math section of the GRE tests the "ability to reason quantitatively and to solve problems in a quantitative setting." Translation: It mostly tests how much you remember from the math courses you took in seventh, eighth, and ninth grades. That means good news for you: GRE math is easier than SAT math. As you might know, many people study little or no math in college. If the GRE tested "college-level" math, everyone but math majors would bomb. So, junior high it is. By brushing up on the modest amount of math you need to know for the test, you can significantly increase your GRE math score.

So, ETS is limited to the math that nearly everyone has studied: arithmetic, basic algebra, basic geometry, and basic statistics. There's no calculus (or even precalculus), no trigonometry, and no major-league algebra or geometry. Because of these limitations, ETS has to resort to tricks and traps in order to create hard problems. Even the most difficult GRE math problems are typically based on pretty simple principles; what makes some difficult is that the simple principles are disguised with tricky wording. In a way, this is more of a reading test than a math test.

MATH VOCABULARY

Vocabulary in the math section? Well, if the math section is just a reading test, then in order to understand what you read, you have to know the language, right?

Quick—what's an integer? Is 0 even or odd? How many even prime numbers are there? These terms look familiar, but it's been a while, right? (We've sorted the terms in alphabetical order, but feel free to skip around.) Review the following:

1. **Consecutive**—Integers listed in order of increasing value without any integers missing in between. For example: –3, –2, –1, 0, 1, 2, 3.

2. **Decimals**—When you're adding or subtracting decimals, just pretend you're dealing with money. Simply line up the decimal points and proceed as you would if the decimal points weren't there.

$$
\begin{array}{r}
34.500 \\
87.000 \\
123.456 \\
+ \ \ 0.980 \\
\hline
245.936
\end{array}
$$

Subtraction works the same way:

$$
\begin{array}{r}
17.66 \\
- \ \ 3.20 \\
\hline
14.46
\end{array}
$$

To multiply, just do it as if the decimal points weren't there. Then put the point in afterward, counting the total number of digits to the right of the decimal points in the numbers you are multiplying. Then, place the decimal point in your solution so that you have the same number of digits to the right of it:

$$
\begin{array}{r}
3.451 \\
\times \ \ \ \ 8.9 \\
\hline
30.7139
\end{array}
$$

Except for placing the decimal point, we did exactly what we would have done if we had been multiplying 3,451 and 89.

To divide, set up the problem as a fraction, then, move the decimal point in the divisor all the way to the right. You must then move the decimal point in the other number the same number of spaces to the right. For example:

$$
\frac{24}{1.25} = \frac{2400}{125} = 19.2
$$

3. **Difference**—the result of subtraction.

4. **Digit**—The numbers 0, 1, 2, 3, 4, 5, 6, 7, 8, and 9. Just think of them as the numbers on your phone dial. The number 189.75 has five digits: 1, 8, 9, 7, and 5. Five is the hundredths digit, 7 is the tenths digit, 9 is the units digit, 8 is the tens digit, and 1 is the hundreds digit.

5. **Divisible**—Capable of being divided with no remainder. An integer is divisible by 2 if its units digit is divisible by 2. An integer is divisible by 3 if the sum of its digits is divisible by 3. An integer is divisible by 5 if its units digit is either 0 or 5. An integer is divisible by 10 if its units digit is 0.

6. **Even/odd**—An even number is any integer that can be divided evenly by 2 (like 4, 8, and 22); any integer is even if its units digit is even. An odd number is any integer that can't be divided evenly by 2 (like 3, 7, and 31); any integer is odd if its units digit is odd. Even + even = even; odd + odd = even; even + odd = odd; even × even = even; odd × odd = odd; even × odd = even. If you're not sure, just put in your own numbers. Don't confuse odd and even with positive and negative. Fractions are neither even nor odd.

7. **Exponent**—Exponents are a sort of mathematical shorthand. Instead of writing (2)(2)(2)(2), we can write 2^4. The little 4 is called an "exponent" and the big 2 is called a "base."

HERE ARE SOME RULES ABOUT EXPONENTS

Raising a number greater than 1 to a power greater than 1 results in a bigger number. For example, $2^2 = 4$.

Raising a fraction between 0 and 1 to a power greater than 1 results in a smaller number. For example, $(\frac{1}{2})^2 = \frac{1}{4}$.

A negative number raised to an even power becomes positive. For example, $(-2)^2 = 4$.

A negative number raised to an odd power remains negative. For example, $(-2)^3 = -8$.

When you see a number raised to an negative exponent, just put a 1 over it and get rid of the negative sign. For example, $(2)^{-2} = (\frac{1}{2})^2$, which $= \frac{1}{4}$.

You probably won't have to worry about adding or subtracting exponents, but you might be asked to multiply or divide. Just remember this phrase: *When in doubt, expand it out.* In other words:

$$2^2 \times 2^4 = (2 \times 2)(2 \times 2 \times 2 \times 2) = 2 \times 2 \times 2 \times 2 \times 2 \times 2 = 2^6$$

Same thing with division

$$2^6 \div 2^2 = (2 \times 2 \times 2 \times 2 \times 2 \times 2) \div (2 \times 2) = 2 \times 2 \times 2 \times 2 = 2^4$$

And don't forget PEMDAS (if you don't remember what PEMDAS is, see number 14):

$$(4^5)^2 = (4 \times 4 \times 4 \times 4 \times 4)(4 \times 4 \times 4 \times 4 \times 4) = 4 \times 4 \times 4 \times 4 \times 4 \times 4 \times 4 \times 4 \times 4 \times 4 = 4^{10}$$

8. **Factor**—a is a factor of b if b can be divided by a without leaving a remainder. For example, 1, 2, 3, 4, 6, and 12 are all factors of 12. All numbers, even prime numbers, have at least two factors. They are one and the number itself. How many times does 12 go into 12? It goes in once with nothing left over.

9. **Fractions**—A fraction is just shorthand for division. On the GRE, you'll probably be asked to compare, add, subtract, multiply, and divide them. In multiplication, you just go straight across:

$$\frac{4}{5} \times \frac{2}{3} = \frac{8}{15}$$

In division, you multiply by the second fraction's reciprocal; in other words, turn the second fraction upside down. In other words, put its denominator (the bottom number) over its numerator (the top number), then multiply:

$$\frac{4}{5} \div \frac{2}{3} = \frac{4}{5} \times \frac{3}{2} = \frac{12}{10} = \frac{6}{5}$$

If you were asked to compare $\frac{3}{7}$ and $\frac{7}{14}$, all you have to do is multiply diagonally up from each denominator, as shown:

$$42 \overset{\nwarrow}{\underset{\searrow}{}} \frac{3}{7} \bowtie \frac{7}{14} \overset{\nearrow}{} 49$$

Now, just compare 42 to 49. Because 49 is bigger, that means $\frac{7}{14}$ is the bigger fraction. This technique is called the *Bowtie*.

You can also use the Bowtie to add or subtract fractions with different denominators (because to add or subtract, the fractions need the same denominator). Just multiply the denominators of the two fractions, and then multiply diagonally up from each denominator, as shown:

$$\frac{3}{4} + \frac{2}{7} = {}^{21}\frac{3}{4} \bowtie \frac{2}{7}^{8} = \frac{21}{28} + \frac{8}{28} = \frac{29}{28}$$

$$\frac{3}{4} - \frac{2}{7} = {}^{21}\frac{3}{4} \bowtie \frac{2}{7}^{8} = \frac{21}{28} - \frac{8}{28} = \frac{13}{28}$$

If the denominators are the same, you don't need the Bowtie. You just keep the same denominator and add or subtract the numerators:

$$\frac{1}{9} + \frac{2}{9} + \frac{4}{9} = \frac{1+2+4}{9} = \frac{7}{9}$$

$$\frac{7}{9} - \frac{4}{9} - \frac{2}{9} = \frac{7-4-2}{9} = \frac{1}{9}$$

10. **Integer**—The integers are the "big places" on the number line: –5, –4, –3, –2, –1, 0, 1, 2, 3, 4, 5, 6. Note that fractions, such as $\frac{1}{2}$, are not integers. Neither are decimals.

11. **Multiple**—A multiple of a number is that number multiplied by an integer other than 0. 10, 20, 30, 40, 50, and 60 are all multiples of 10.

12. **Order of operations**—Also known as PEMDAS, or Please Excuse My Dear Aunt Sally. Parentheses > Exponents > Multiplication = Division > Addition = Subtraction. This is the order in which the operations are to be performed. For example:

$$10 - (6 - 5) - (3 + 3) - 3 =$$

Start with the parentheses. The expression inside the first pair of parentheses, $6 - 5$, equals 1. The expression inside the second pair equals 6. Now rewrite the problem as follows:

$$10 - 1 - 6 - 3 =$$
$$9 - 6 - 3 =$$
$$3 - 3 =$$
$$= 0$$

Here's another example:

Say you were asked to compare $(3 \times 2)^2$ and $(3) (2^2)$. $(3 \times 2)^2 = 6^2$, or 36, and $(3) (2^2) = 3 \times 4$, or 12.

Note that with multiplication and division, you just go left to right (hence the "=" sign in the description of PEMDAS above). Same with addition and subtraction. In other words, if the only operations you have to perform are multiplication and division, you don't have to do all multiplication first, because they are equivalent operations. Just go left to right.

13. **Positive/negative**—Positive integers get bigger as they move away from 0 (6 is bigger than 5); negative integers get smaller as they move away from zero (–6 is smaller than –5). Positive $\times$ positive = positive; negative $\times$ negative = positive; positive $\times$ negative = negative. Be careful not to confuse positive and negative with odd and even.

14. **Prime**—A prime number is a number that is evenly divisible only by itself and by 1. Zero and 1 are not prime numbers, and 2 is the only even prime number. Other prime numbers include 3, 5, 7, 11, and 13 (but there are many more).

15. **Probability**—Probability is equal to the outcome you're looking for divided by the total outcomes. If it is impossible for something to happen, the probability of it happening is equal to 0. If something is certain to happen, the probability is equal to 1. If it is possible for something to happen, but not necessary, the probability is between 0 and 1, otherwise known as a fraction. For example, if you flip a coin, what's the probability that it will land on "heads"? One out of two, or $\frac{1}{2}$. What is the probability that it won't land on "heads"? One out of two, or $\frac{1}{2}$. If you flip a coin nine times, what's the probability that the coin will land on "heads" on the tenth flip? One out of two, or $\frac{1}{2}$. Previous flips do not affect anything.

17. **Product**—the result of multiplication.

18. **Quotient**—the result of division.

19. **Reducing fractions**—To reduce a fraction, "cancel" or cross out factors that are common to both the numerator and the denominator. For example, to reduce $\frac{18}{24}$, just divide both 18 and 24 by the biggest common factor, 6. That leaves you with $\frac{3}{4}$. If you couldn't think of 6, both 18 and 24 are even, so just start cutting them in half (or by thirds) till you can't go any further. And remember—you cannot reduce numbers across an equal sign (=), a plus sign (+), or a minus sign (–).

20. **Remainder**—The remainder is the number left over when one integer cannot be divided evenly by another. The remainder is always an integer. Remember grade school math class? It's the number that came after the big "R." For example, the remainder when 7 is divided by 4 is **3** because 4 goes into 7 one time with 3 left over. ETS likes remainder questions because you can't do them on your calculator.

21. **Square root**—The sign $\sqrt{}$ indicates the square root of a number. For example, $\sqrt{2}$ means that something squared equals 2. You can't add or subtract square roots unless they have the same number under the root sign ($\sqrt{2} + \sqrt{3}$ does *not* equal $\sqrt{5}$, but $\sqrt{2} + \sqrt{2} = 2\sqrt{2}$). You can multiply and divide them just like regular integers:

$$\sqrt{2} \times \sqrt{3} = \sqrt{6}$$
$$\sqrt{6} \div \sqrt{3} = \sqrt{2}$$

You will have a square root symbol on your calculator, but it is often easier if you recognize the common ones on site. Here are a few square roots to remember that might come in handy:

$$\sqrt{1} = 1$$
$$\sqrt{2} = 1.4$$
$$\sqrt{3} = 1.\dot{7}$$
$$\sqrt{4} = 2$$

Note: If you're told that $x^2 = 16$, then $x = \pm 4$. You must be especially careful to remember this on quantitative comparison questions. But if you're asked for the value $\sqrt{16}$, you are being asked for the positive root only, so the answer is 4. A square root is always positive.

22. **Standard deviation**—The standard deviation of a set is a measure of the set's variation from its mean. You'll rarely, if ever, have to actually calculate it, so just remember this: The bigger the standard deviation, the more widely dispersed the values are. The smaller the standard deviation, the more closely grouped the values in a set are around the mean. For example, the standard deviation of the numbers 6, 0, and 6 is bigger than the standard deviation of the numbers 4, 4, and 4, because 6, 0, and 6 are more widely dispersed than 4, 4, and 4.

23. **Sum**—The result of addition.

24. **Zero**—An integer that's neither positive nor negative, but is even. The sum of 0 and any other number is that other number; the product of 0 and any other number is 0.

QUANTITATIVE COMPARISON

There are four question formats on the math section: five-choice problem-solving questions, four-choice quantitative comparisons (or quant comps), All that Apply consisting of three up to a possible eith answer choices, and Numeric Entry in which there are no answer choices and you have to supply your own answer. A quant comp is a math question that consists of two quantities, one in Quantity A and one in Quantity B. You are to compare the two quantities and choose:

(A) Quantity A is greater.

(B) Quantity B is greater.

(C) The quantities are equal.

(D) The relationship cannot be determined from the information given.

In this book, we're going to phrase the answer choices exactly that way, although on your test it will be slightly different (but it will mean the same thing).

Quant comps have only four answer choices. That's great: A blind guess has one chance in four of being correct. Always write A, B, C, D (but no E) on your scratch paper so you can cross off wrong answer choices as you go. The content of quant comp problems is drawn from the same basic arithmetic, algebra, and geometry concepts that are used on GRE math problems in other formats. In general, then, you'll apply the same techniques that you use on other types of math questions. Still, quant comps do require a few special techniques of their own.

The Peculiar Behavior of Choice (D)

Any problem containing only numbers must have a single solution. Therefore, the fourth bubble, or choice (D), can be eliminated immediately on all such problems. For example:

Quantity A	Quantity B
$\dfrac{2}{3}$	$\dfrac{3}{4}$

- ○ Quantity A is greater.
- ○ Quantity B is greater.
- ○ The two quantities are equal.
- ○ The relationship cannot be determined from the information given.

You know the answer can be determined, so the answer could never be choice (D). So right off the bat, as soon as you see a quant comp that involves only numbers, you can eliminate (D) on your scratch paper. The answer to this one is (B), by the way. Use the Bowtie, so you end up with 8 versus 9.

Compare Before You Calculate

You don't always have to figure out what the exact values would be in both columns before you compare them. The prime directive is to compare the two columns. Finding ETS's answer frequently is merely a matter of simplifying, reducing, factoring, or unfactoring. For example:

Quantity A	Quantity B
$\dfrac{1}{17} + \dfrac{1}{8} + \dfrac{1}{5}$	$\dfrac{1}{5} + \dfrac{1}{17} + \dfrac{1}{7}$

- ○ Quantity A is greater.
- ○ Quantity B is greater.
- ○ The two quantities are equal.
- ○ The relationship cannot be determined from the information given.

The first thing to do is eliminate choice (D), because there are only numbers here. Then, notice that there are fractions in common to both columns; both contain $\dfrac{1}{17}$ and $\dfrac{1}{5}$. If the same numbers are in both columns, they can't make a difference to the total quantity. So just cross them off (after copying down the problem on your scratch paper, of course). Now, what's left? In Quantity A we have $\dfrac{1}{8}$, and in Quantity B we have $\dfrac{1}{7}$. All we have to do now is compare $\dfrac{1}{8}$ to $\dfrac{1}{7}$. Use the Bowtie and we get choice (B).

BE STRATEGIC WHEN DOING ALGEBRA

BE STRATEGIC WHEN DOING ALGEBRA

A normal person might say, "I have ten dollars. I'm going to buy three pieces of candy, and each one costs 50 cents. How much change do I get?" The normal answer would be $8.50. ETS is not normal. They will ask you the same question, but when they ask it, they say, "I have x dollars. I'm going to buy y pieces of candy and each piece costs z cents. Now how much change do I get ($z - xy$ would be a tempting answer choice for this question, but wrong)? This is called algebra. In algebra, normal numbers are replaced with abstract symbols (who has ever heard of z dollars?). We know the logic of numbers so well, that finding an answer requires nothing more than common sense, but with symbols it's different. You never really know you have the right answer with symbols, and then, because they don't follow common sense, you have to learn all sorts of rules to tell you what you're allowed to do with them. Anytime the GRE gives us algebra, all we're going to do is take the symbols out, and put the numbers back in. When you do this, the only math functions you ever have to perform are addition, subtraction, multiplication, and division. Here's an example:

> Kyle has four fewer toys than Scott,
> but seven more toys than Jody. If
> Kyle has k toys, then how many toys
> do Scott and Jody have together?
>
> ○ $2k + 11$
> ○ $2k + 7$
> ○ $2k + 3$
> ○ $2k - 3$
> ○ $2k - 11$

Step 1—Recognize the opportunity. The minute you see variables in the question and variables in the answers, you know you can Plug In.

Step 2—Engage the hand. As soon as you recognize the problem as a Plug In, write A, B, C, D, and E in a column in the upper left corner of your scratch paper.

Step 3—Plug In. Who's ever heard of k toys? Give k a number. Let's say $k = 10$. Write this down on your scratch paper. Now work the problem. Kyle has four fewer toys than Scott. If Kyle has 10, then Scott has 14. Write down $s = 14$ on your scratch paper. Kyle has seven more toys than Jodi, so write $j = 3$ on your scratch paper.

Step 4—Identify and circle your target number. The target number is the number the question asks you to find. In this case, the question asks us, "How many toys do Scott and Jody have together?" Well, Scott has 14 and Jody has 3, so our target number is 17. Write it down and circle it.

Step 5—Use POE. Now check all answer choices. Anywhere you see a k, Plug In 10. You're shooting for a 17.

(A) $2(10) + 11$—Nope. Cross it off.

(B) $2(10) + 7$—Nope. Cross it off.

(C) $2(10) + 3$—Nope. Cross it off.

(D) $2(10) - 3 = 17$. This looks good, but always check all answer choices.

(E) $2(10) - 11$—Nope.

The answer is (D). Here is what your scratch paper should look like:

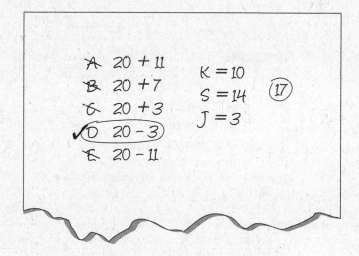

When Plugging In for variables, there are a few things to keep in mind:

a. **Do all work on your scratch paper.** When you're done you should always see all terms labeled, a target number circled, and all answer choices checked.

b. **Plug In nice, happy numbers that make your life easier.** If you Plug In a number and the math gets creepy, don't sweat it; just change your Plug In. Avoid Plugging In 0, 1, the same number for multiple variables, or numbers that you find in the question. They're not necessarily wrong; they're just likely to yield more than one answer choice.

c. **Check to see if more than one answer choice works.** If so, Plug In a new number, find a new target number, and check only the answer choices that remain.

Plugging In on Quant Comp

So you're sitting in your cubical at the test center, and this question pops up:

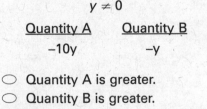

$$y \neq 0$$

Quantity A	Quantity B
$-10y$	$-y$

○ Quantity A is greater.
○ Quantity B is greater.
○ The two quantities are equal.
○ The relationship cannot be determined from the information given.

Step 1—Recognize the opportunity. The first thing you see is that it's a quant comp problem. The second thing you see is variables. This is a Plug In. This all takes about 4 seconds to process.

Step 2—Engage the hand. On the fifth second, reach for your scratch paper. When you see variables on quant comp, make the set-up. It looks like this:

Step 3—Plug In something happy and use POE. Throw a nice happy number in there. Let's make $y = 2$. Now, when $y = 2$, then Quantity A is –20, and Quantity B is –2. Write these down in columns

as you go. Which one is bigger? Quantity B. Remember what the answer choices mean on quant comp questions. Choice (A) means that the value in Quantity A is always bigger, no matter what. Here we have a case where we've followed all of the rules and A is not bigger, so choice (A) can't be the answer. Cross off choice (A). Since they're not the same, you can cross off (C) as well.

Step 4—Keep Plugging In according to ZONE F. On a regular Plug In we always want to Plug In nice, happy numbers. On a quant comp Plug In, we have to Plug In the weird stuff. ZONE F is a list of the weird stuff. It stands for Zero, One, Negatives, Extra big/small numbers, and Fractions. Be strategic. When you look at this problem, how can you mess with it? The problem asks about negative numbers, so try Plugging In a negative. Make $y = -2$. Now, Quantity A is 20, and Quantity B is 2. A is bigger so cross of choice (B). Since only (D) is left, that must be the answer.

Here's what your scratch paper should look like:

Always keep Plugging In until you've eliminated choices (A), (B), and (C), or you've tried everything on ZONE F. If you've tried everything on ZONE F and either (A), (B), or (C) is still standing, then that's your answer.

Let's try one more:

$$0 < x < 10$$
$$0 < y < 1$$

Quantity A	Quantity B
$x - y$	9

○ Quantity A is greater.
○ Quantity B is greater.
○ The two quantities are equal.
○ The relationship cannot be determined from the information given.

Step 1—Recognize the opportunity. Quant comp? Yup. Variables? Yup.

Step 2—Engage the hand. Make your set-up on your scratch paper.

Step 3—Plug In. Here we have ranges for x and y, so let's Plug In our biggest x and our smallest y. Make $x = 9$ and $y = .1$. In Quantity A we have 8.9, and in Quantity B we have 9. Quantity B is bigger, so cross off choices (A) and (C). Now let's try our smallest x with our biggest y. Make $x = .1$ and $y = 9$. In Quantity A we have .1. In Quantity B we still have 9. Quantity B is still bigger. Now is a good time to use the ZONE F checklist. We can't Plug In zero. We tried 1. We can't Plug In a negative. We used large and small numbers. What about fractions? We Plugged In fractions for y, but what about x? There is no law that says that we can Plug In only integers. Try $x = 9.9$ and $y = .1$. In Quantity A we get 9.8, and in Quantity B we still have 9. Quantity A is bigger, so cross off choice (B) and pick choice (C). Getting the hang of it?

Must Be

Take a look at this question:

> The positive difference between the squares of any two consecutive integers, x and x + 1, must be
>
> ○ the square of an integer
> ○ a multiple of 5
> ○ an even integer
> ○ an odd number
> · ○ a prime number

The phrase "must be" is a lot like the word "always" we just saw in the quant comps. This is like asking, which of the following must always be true, no matter what? We can treat these the same way.

Step 1—Recognize the opportunity. The phrase "must be" in a question is a trigger that provokes a specific action. Sensitize yourself to it.

Step 2—Engage the hand. The minute you see the phrase "must be," make your set-up. Variables go across the top, and answer choices go across the bottom. It looks like this:

$$x = \qquad x = \qquad x =$$
$$y = \qquad y = \qquad y =$$

A
B
C
D
E

Step 3—Plug In and use POE. Start with something nice and happy. Try $x = 2$. If $x = 2$, then $x + 1 = 3$. The squares are 4 and 9, and the positive difference is 5. Remember to always park your set-ups on the left-hand side of your scratch paper so that the right-hand side is free for any scratch work you might have to do. (A) does not work. Put an x next to it and cross off (A). (B) works. Give it a check. (C) does not work. Put and x next to it and cross off (C). (D) works. Give it a check. (E) works. Give it a check.

Step 4—Keep Plugging In. "Must be" is really code for "Plug In more than once." Keep going until there's only one left. Try $x = 10$. Our squares are 100 and 121. The difference is 21. You need to check only answer choices that are still standing. (B) does not work. Put an x next to it and cross it off. (D) works. Give it a check. (E) does not work. Give it an x and cross it off. The only one left is (D). That's our answer. Your scratch paper should look like this:

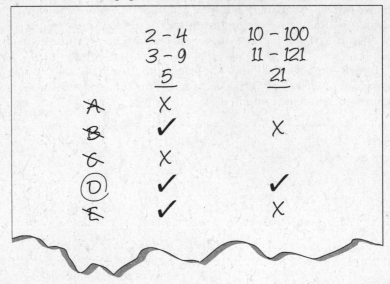

PITA

There is one more kind of Plugging In. It's called PITA which stands for Plugging In The Answers. It is one of the most powerful types of Plugging In because it can take some of the hardest problems on the GRE and turn them into simple arithmetic. The hardest thing about this technique, however, is remembering to use it. Let's look at a question:

> Two positive integers, x and y, have a difference of 15. If the smaller integer, y, is $\frac{5}{8}$ of x, then what is the value of y?
>
> ○ 40
> ○ 25
> ○ 20
> ○ 15
> ○ 10

Step 1—Recognize the opportunity. There are three signs that you can Plug In the answers:

a. The question contains the phrase "how much...," "how many....," or "what is the value of...."

b. You have specific numbers in the answer choices in ascending or descending order.

c. You are tempted to design or write your own algebraic formula to solve the problem.

Step 2—Engage the hand. The minute you recognize the opportunity, list the answer choices in the upper left corner of your scratch paper. In this case, list 40, 25, 20, 15, and 10 in a vertical column in the upper left hand side of your scratch paper.

Step 3—Label the First Column. The question asks, "What is the value of y?" The answer choices, therefore, represent possible values for y. Label that first column "y."

Step 4—Assume (C) to be correct. If $y = 20$, what else do we know?

Step 5—Work the problem in bite-sized pieces. Make a new column for every step. The problem tells us that y is $\dfrac{5}{8}$ of x. So if $y = 20$, then $x = 32$. Make a column labeled "x" and write 32 in the column next to the 20.

Step 6—Use POE. How do we know if (C) is the correct answer? There must be a difference of 15 between x and y. With choice (C) there is only a difference of 12. Cross off choice (C). For a bigger difference we will need bigger numbers, so cross off choices (D) and (E) as well. Now, not only are we down to a 50/50 shot, but we also have a little spreadsheet designed specifically to calculate the answer to this problem. Just fill in the cells. If $x = 25$, then $y = 40$. The difference is 15, and we have an answer. When you're Plugging In The Answers, only one can work. So when you get one that works, you're done. Here's what your scratch paper should look like after this problem:

Let's try one more.

Vicken, Roger, and Adam went to
buy a $90 radio. If Roger agrees to
pay twice as much as Adam and
Vicken agrees to pay three times
as much as Roger, how much must
Roger pay?

○ $10
○ $20
○ $30
○ $45
○ $65

Step 1—Recognize the opportunity. The question asks "How much must Roger pay?"

Step 2—Engage the hand. List the answer choices, $10, $20, $30, $45, and $65 on your scratch paper.

Step 3—Label the first column. What do those numbers represent? The amount Roger pays.

Step 4—Assume (C) to be correct. Reread the problem, but assume that it says that Roger pays $30.

Step 5—Work the problem in bite-size pieces. Make a new column for every step. If Roger pays $30, then Adam pays $15. Make a column for Adam. Vicken pays $90, so make a column for Vicken.

Step 6—Use POE. Now we have a problem because the whole radio costs $90. Cross off choice (C). We also know that (C) is too big, so cross off (D) and (E). Now fill in the columns for answer choice (B). If Roger pays $20, then Adam pays $10, and Vicken pays $60. All three together pay $90, which is exactly what they should be paying, so we are done and the answer is (B).

Your scratch paper should look something like this:

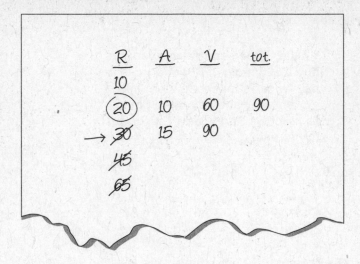

There are four kinds of Plugging In we've reviewed here:

1. **Plugging In for variables.** When you see variables in the question and the answer choices, you can Plug In. Make sure you have your terms labeled, your target number circled, and all answer choices checked.

2. **Quant comp Plug In.** When you see quant comp and variables, make your set-up. Plug In according to ZONE F, eliminating as you go.

3. **Must be.** "Must be" is code for "Plug In more than once." Make your set-up with variables across the top and answer choices down the side. Plug In according to ZONE F, eliminating as you go.

4. **PITA.** When the question asks, How much? How many? or What is the value of? you know you can Plug In The Answers. Label the first column, start with choice (C), and make a new column for every step. When you find one that works, you're done.

FIND THE MISSING PIECES IN GEOMETRY

FIND THE MISSING PIECES IN GEOMETRY

Geometry on the GRE is really like a series of brainteasers. It is your job to find the missing piece of information. They will always give you four out of five pieces of information, and you will always be able to find the fifth. There are only about a half dozen concepts that show up. Once you learn to recognize them, you should be able to handle any problems you might see. The basic problems are made up of parallel lines, triangles, circles, and quadrilaterals.

First, a few basics:

1. **Line**—A line (which can be thought of as a perfectly flat angle) is a 180-degree angle.

2. **Perpendicular**—When two lines are perpendicular to each other, their intersection forms four 90-degree angles.

3. **Right angle**—Ninety-degree angles are also called right angles. A right angle on the GRE is identified by a little box at the intersection of the angle's sides:

4. **Vertical angles**—Vertical angles are the angles across from each other that are formed by the intersection of lines. Vertical angles are equal.

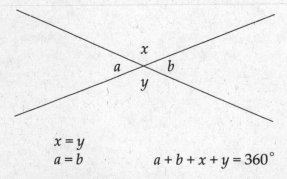

$$x = y$$
$$a = b \qquad a + b + x + y = 360°$$

4. **Parallel lines**—First, never assume two lines are parallel unless they tell you or you can prove it. When you see the symbol for parallel lines, however, there's generally only one thing interesting about parallel lines. When you see a pair of parallel lines intersected by a third, two kinds of angles are formed: big ones and small ones. All big angles are equal to all big angles and all small angles are equal to all small angles. Any big + any small = 180 degrees. When you see the symbol for parallel lines, always and automatically identify the big angles and the small angles. They are almost assuredly going to come into play. Otherwise, why make them parallel?

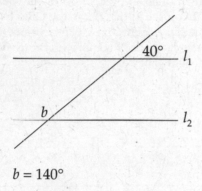

$$b = 140°$$

riangles

ou know the basics about triangles. All of the angles add up to 180. he largest side is opposite the largest angle, just as the smallest side 3 opposite the smallest angle. The formula for the area of a triangle 3 $A = \dfrac{1}{2}(b)(h)$. An equilateral triangle is one in which all three sides, and hence, all three angles, are the same. The angles on an equilateral riangle are all 60°.° An isosceles triangle is one in which two of the 3ides are the equal. Naturally, sides opposite equal angles are equal in ength and vice versa.

A lesser-known rule is that of the third side. The third side of a triangle is always less than the sum of the other two sides, but greater than the difference.

The most frequent triangles you will see are right triangles. A right triangle has one 90° angle and two smaller ones. If you know the length two sides of a right triangle, you can always find the length of the third because of the Pythagorean theorem, which says that $a^2 + b^2 = c^2$ where c is the hypotenuse (that means that c represents the longest side, which is the one opposite the 90° angle, which is always the largest angle). The Pythagorean theorem tells us that if you add the squares of the lengths of the two shorter sides of a right triangle, it will add up to the square of the longest side.

It's good to understand how the Pythagorean theorem works, but you rarely need it because there are three kinds of right triangles that come up all of the time. Once you recognize them, you can save yourself some math. So, if you see a triangle on the GRE, be suspicious. If you see a triangle and it is a right triangle, be extremely suspicious. It is likely to be one of three kinds of common right triangles that you should recognize on sight. They are:

Pythagorean Triple—

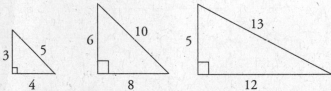

The Pythagorean theorem will work on any right triangle, but on a Pythagorean triple, a^2, b^2 and c^2 are all integers. If you see a triangle, and it's a right triangle and you see sides of 3 and 4, you're done. If you see a long side of 13 and a short side of 5, you're done. Sensitize yourself to these numbers and recognize them on sight.

Right Isosceles—

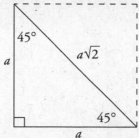

If you have a square (all sides are equal, all angles are 90°) and you cut it in half on the diagonal, you end up with the triangle you see above. The two sides of the square remain equal. If each side of the square is x, then the diagonal of the square (the same as the hypotenuse of the right triangle) is $x\sqrt{2}$. If you see a triangle and there is a $\sqrt{2}$ in the problem somewhere, you know what you're looking for. This means that you also always know the length of the diagonal of a square if you know one side of the square or the area of the square.

30-60-90—

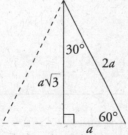

If you take an equilateral triangle and cut it in half, you create the smaller triangle you see above. The angle that never changed, remains 60°. The angle at the top got cut in half and is now 30°. The angle at the base is 90°. One side of the triangle you cut in half, and one side you left the same. If the small side of the new triangle is x, then the big side (opposite the 90°) angle is $2x$. The side in the middle, opposite the 60° angle, is $x\sqrt{3}$. This is an especially useful triangle because it means that you always know the area of an equilateral triangle because you always know the height. The height of any equilateral triangle is one half of one side times the square root of three. If you see a right triangle and you see a $\sqrt{3}$ hanging around the problem anywhere, look for this triangle.

Circles

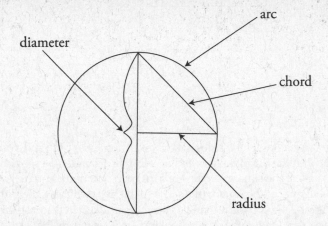

Circle Facts

- All circles contain 360°.

- The radius of a circle is the distance from the center to the outer edge.

- The diameter is the longest distance within a circle and passes through the center. The diameter is twice the radius.

- The formula for area of a circle is $A = \pi r^2$.

- The formula for circumference (perimeter) of a circle is πd, or $2\pi r$.

With circles, once you know the radius, you know everything. You should be comfortable going from circumference to radius to area and back. Remember that pi equals approximately 3.14 should you need to estimate something, but as a general rule, leave it as pi.

Quadrilaterals

1. **Four-sided figure**—Any figure with four sides has 360 degrees. That includes rectangles, squares, and parallelograms (four-sided figures made out of two sets of parallel lines).

2. **Parallelogram**—A four-sided figure made from two sets of parallel lines. The opposite angles are equal, and the big angle plus the small angle add up to 180 degrees.

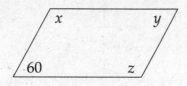

$$x = 120°, y = 60°, z = 120°$$

3. **Rectangle**—A four-sided figure where the opposite sides are parallel and all angles are 90 degrees. The area of a rectangle is length times width ($A = lw$).

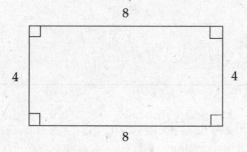

$$\text{perimeter} = 4 + 8 + 4 + 8 = 24$$
$$\text{area} = 8 \times 4 = 32$$

4. **Square**—A square is a rectangle with four equal sides. The area is the length of any side times itself, which is to say, the length of any side squared ($A - s^?$).

A Few Other Odds and Ends

1. **Coordinate geometry**—This involves a grid where the horizontal line is the *x*-axis and the vertical line is the *y*-axis. The *x*-coordinate always comes first, and the *y*-coordinate always comes second.

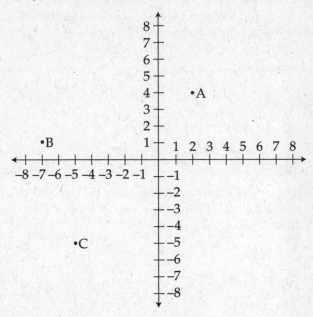

Point A on the diagram above is (2, 4) because the *x*-coordinate is 2 over from the origin (0, 0) and the *y*-coordinate is 4 above the origin. Point B is (–7, 1). Point C is (–5, –5).

2. **Inscribed**—A figure is inscribed within another figure if points on the edge of the enclosed figure touch the outer figure.

3. **Perimeter**—The perimeter of a rectangle, square, parallelogram, triangle, or any sided figure is the sum of the lengths of the sides:

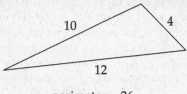

perimeter = 26

4. **Slope**—In coordinate geometry, the equation of a line, or slope, is $y = mx + b$, where the x and the y are points on the line, b stands for the "y-intercept," or the point at which the line crosses the y-axis, and m is the actual slope of the line, or the change in y divided by the change in x. *Note:* Sometimes ETS uses an a instead of an m.

5. **Surface area**—The surface area of a rectangular box is equal to the sum of the areas of all of its sides. In other words, if you had a box whose dimensions were 2 by 3 by 4, there would be two sides that are 2 by 3 (area of 6), two sides that are 3 by 4 (area of 12), and two sides that are 2 by 4 (area of 8). So, the surface area would be 6 + 6 + 12 + 12 + 8 + 8, which is 52.

6. **Volume**—The volume of a rectangular solid is $l \times w \times h$ (length times width times height). The volume of a circular cylinder is πr^2 (the area of the circle that forms the base) times the height (in other words, $\pi r^2 h$).

The Basic Approach

Step 1—Engage the hand. You will need to work with your shapes and fill in lots of little pieces of information, so it is important to get your shape drawn on your scratch paper. Try to draw the shape to scale, but remember to base your information upon what you're told, not necessarily what you're shown on screen (on-screen shapes can be misleading). Drawing your shape is particularly important when you're not actually given a picture of the shape as part of the problem.

Step 2—Fill in what you know. The problem will give you various pieces of information. It might give you an angle or two, the length of a side, or a relationship between two elements, for example. Park all of that information on your drawing.

Step 3—Make deductions. If a problem gives you two angles in a triangle, you can calculate the third. Always do this as a matter of good test-taking habits. The information you're given will allow you to make some deductions. Sometimes these deductions alone are enough to lead you to the correct answer.

Step 4—Write relevant formulas. Geometry on the GRE is all about finding the missing piece of information. Writing down the formulas you need will help you to organize the information you have and will also tell you which pieces you are missing. This is a trigger and response relationship, just like other parts of the test. When you are working with triangles and you see the word "area," automatically write down the formula for the area of a triangle. You will end up needing it sooner or later, and it will give you a place to put some of the information you're given. This is true for any problem that involves a formula.

Step 5—Drop heights/draw lines. When taking your test, you always want to be doing, not thinking. When you get stuck on a geometry problem, first walk away and do a few other problems to distract your brain. When you come back, you need to find another way to view the problem. This is where Step 5 comes in. Try dropping the height of a triangle or parallelogram, drawing in a few extra radii in a circle, or subdividing a strange shape to make two shapes you recognize. Engage your hand and do something. Staring at the problem isn't going to make it easier.

Here's an example:

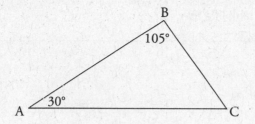

In the triangle above, if BC = $4\sqrt{2}$, then AB =

○ 6

○ $4\sqrt{3}$

○ 8

○ $4\sqrt{6}$

○ 10

Step 1—Draw your shape.

Step 2—Fill in what you know. BC is $4\sqrt{2}$. This is a highly suspicious number. No one, not even ETS, randomly decides to make one side of a triangle include a square root. There must be a reason. What kind of triangle uses a $\sqrt{2}$?

Step 3—Make deductions. We know the third angle. It's 45 degrees. Now you have a 45-degree angle and a $\sqrt{2}$ in the same problem. There must be a right isosceles triangle in here somewhere.

Step 4—Write relevant formulas. This problem doesn't call for any formulas.

Step 5—Drop heights/draw lines. Anytime you drop the height of a triangle, a right angle is formed by the intersection of the height and the base of the triangle. Look at that. There's your right isosceles! The angle at the top is 45 degrees too. If the hypotenuse is $4\sqrt{2}$, then each of the smaller sides is 4. Plug them into your drawing. On the other side we have another triangle. This one has a 30° angle, a 90° angle. You don't even have to calculate the third angle; it must be 60º.

This is a 30-60-90 triangle, which means that we know the ratio of the sides. The short side, opposite the 30 degree angle is 4. The long side, opposite the right angle, therefore, must be 8. This is side AB, which is the side we were asked to find. The correct answer is (C). Your scratch paper should look like this:

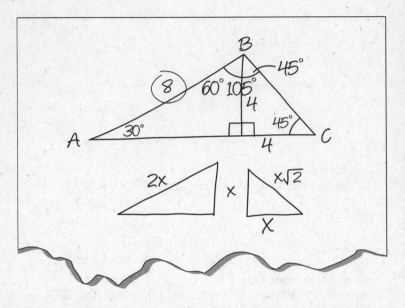

Geometry problems are often like a small piece of knitting. Once you find and tug on the loose thread, the whole thing begins to unravel. The steps are designed to tease out that loose thread.

Geometry on Quant Comp

Quantity A	Quantity B
The area of a square region with perimeter 20	The area of a rectangular region with perimeter 20

○ Quantity A is greater.
○ Quantity B is greater.
○ The two quantities are equal.
○ The relationship cannot be determined from the information given.

When solving a quantitative comparison with variables, you need to always Plug In more than once. The equivalent of Plugging In more than once with a geometry question is drawing your shape more than once. Ask yourself, "Is there more than one way to draw this shape?"

You can set this problem up just like a quant comp Plug In. Quantity A does not change because there is only one way to draw a square. If the perimeter is 20, then one side is 5, and the area is 25. Now draw a rectangle for Quantity B and make the area as small as possible. You could have a long skinny rectangle with long sides of 9 and short sides of 1. The perimeter is 20, but the area is 9. Cross off choices (B) and (C). Now redraw your shape. How big can you make that area? The biggest you could make it is to make a square with sides of five (a square is a rectangle). The perimeter is 20, and the area is 25. Cross off choice (A). Your answer is (D).

Your scratch paper should look something like this:

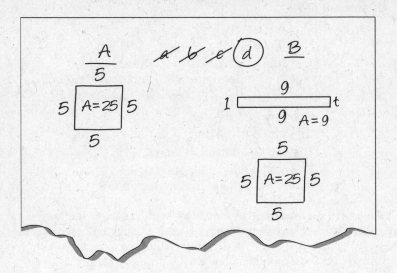

STEP 8

BALLPARK THE EQUATIONS

MATH SENTENCES?

Many GRE math problems involve words and letters, or variables, such as n, x, or y, in equations. It's time to learn how to deal with those.

Solving for One Variable

Any equation with one variable can be solved by manipulating the equation. You get the variables on one side of the equation and the numbers on the other side. To do this, you can add, subtract, multiply, or divide both sides of the equation by the same number. Just remember that anything you do to one side of an equation, you have to do to the other side. Be sure to write down every step. Look at a simple example:

$$4x - 3 = 9$$

You can get rid of negatives by adding something to both sides of the equation, just as you can get rid of positives by subtracting something from both sides of the equation.

$$
\begin{array}{rl}
4x - 3 = & 9 \\
+3 & +3 \\
\hline
4x = & 12
\end{array}
$$

You may already see that $x = 3$. But don't forget to write down that last step. Divide both sides of the equation by 4.

$$\frac{4x}{4} = \frac{12}{4}$$

$$x = 3$$

MORE MATH VOCAB

1. **F.O.I.L.**—F.O.I.L. stands for First, Outer, Inner, Last— the four steps of multiplication when you see two sets of parentheses. Here's an example:

$$(x + 4)(x + 3) = (x + 4)(x + 3)$$

$$= (x \times x) + (x \times 3) + (4 \times x) + (4 \times 3)$$

$$= x^2 + 3x + 4x + 12$$

$$= x^2 + 7x + 12$$

This also works in the opposite direction.

2. **Factoring**—If you rewrite the expression $xy + xz$ as $x(y + z)$, you are said to be factoring the original expression. That is, you take the factor common to both terms of the original expression (x) and "pull it out." This gives you a new, "factored" version of the expression you began with. If you rewrite the expression $x(y + z)$ as $xy + xz$, you are unfactoring the original expression.

3. **Functions**—No, not real mathematical functions. On the GRE, a function is a funny-looking symbol that stands for an operation. For example, say you're told that $m @ n$ is equal to $\frac{m + n}{n - 1}$. What's the value of $4 @ 6$? Just follow directions: $\frac{4 + 6}{6 - 1}$, or $\frac{10}{5}$, or 2. Don't worry that "@" isn't a real mathematical operation; it could have been a "#" or an "&," or any other symbol. The point is, just do what you are told to do.

4. **Inequalities**—Here are the symbols you need to know: ≠ means not equal to; > means greater than; < means less than; ≥ means greater than or equal to; ≤ means less than or equal to. You can manipulate any inequality in the same way you can an equation, with one important difference. For example,

$$10 - 5x > 0$$

You can solve this by subtracting 10 from both sides of the equation, and ending up with $-5x > -10$. Now you have to divide both sides by -5.

$$\frac{-5x}{-5} > \frac{-10}{-5}$$

With inequalities, any time you multiply or divide by a negative number, you have to flip the sign.

$$x < 2$$

5. **Percent**—Percent means "per 100" or "out of 100" or "divided by 100." If your friend finds a dollar and gives you 50 cents, your friend has given you 50 cents out of 100, or $\frac{50}{100}$ of a dollar, or 50 percent of a dollar. When you have to find exact percentages it's much easier if you know how to translate word problems, which lets you express them as equations. Here's a translation "dictionary."

<u>Word</u>	<u>Translates to</u>
percent	/100 (example: 40 percent translates to $\frac{40}{100}$)
is	=
of	×
what	any variable (x, k, b)
what percent	$\frac{x}{100}$

What is 30 percent of 200?

First, translate it, using the "dictionary" above.

$$x = \frac{30}{100} \times 200$$

Now reduce that 100 and 200, and solve for the variable, like this

$$x = 30 \times 2$$

$$x = 60$$

So, 30 percent of 200 is 60.

6. **Percent change**—To find a percentage increase or decrease, first, find the difference between the original number and the new number. Then, divide that by the original number, and then multiply the result by 100. In other words:

$$\text{Percent Change} = \frac{\text{Difference}}{\text{Original}} \times 100$$

For example, if you had to find the percent decrease from 4 to 3, first, figure out what the difference is. The difference, or decrease, from 4 to 3 is 1. The original number is 4. So,

$$\text{Percent Change} = \frac{\text{Difference}}{\text{Original}} \times 100$$

$$\text{Percent Change} = \frac{1}{4} \times 100$$

$$\text{Percent Change} = 25$$

So, the percent decrease from 4 to 3 is 25 percent.

7. **Quadratic equations**—Three equations that sometimes show up on the GRE. Here they are, in their factored and unfactored forms.

Factored form		Unfactored form
$x^2 - y^2$	=	$(x + y)(x - y)$
$(x + y)^2$	=	$x^2 + 2xy + y^2$
$(x - y)^2$	=	$x^2 - 2xy + y^2$

8. **Simultaneous equations**—Two algebraic equations that include the same variables. For example, what if you were told that $5x + 4y = 6$ and $4x + 3y = 5$, and asked what $x + y$ equals? To solve a set of simultaneous equations, you can usually either add them together or subtract one from the other (just remember when you subtract that everything you're subtracting needs to be made negative). Here's what we get when we add them:

$$
\begin{array}{r}
5x + 4y = 6 \\
+\ 4x + 3y = 5 \\
\hline
9x + 7y = 11
\end{array}
$$

A dead end. So, try subtraction.

$$
\begin{array}{r}
5x + 4y = 6 \\
-\ 4x - 3y = -5 \\
\hline
x + y = 1
\end{array}
$$

Eureka. The value of the expression $(x + y)$ is exactly what we're looking for.

BALLPARKING

Say you were asked to find 30 percent of 50. Don't do any math yet. Now let's say that you glance at the answer choices and you see these:

- ○ 5
- ○ 15
- ○ 30
- ○ 80
- ○ 150

Think about it. Whatever 30 percent of 50 is, it must be less than 50, right? So any answer choice greater than 50 can't be right. That means you should eliminate both 80 and 150 right off the bat, without doing any math. You can also eliminate 30, if you think about it. Half, or 50 percent, of 50 is 25, so 30 percent must be less than 25. Congratulations, you've just eliminated three out of five answer choices without doing any math.

What we've just done is known as Ballparking. Ballparking will help you eliminate answer choices and increase your odds of zeroing in on ETS's answer. Remember to eliminate any answer choice that is "out of the ballpark" by crossing them off on your scratch paper (remember, you'll be writing down A, B, C, D, E for each question).

Charts

Ballparking will also help you on the few chart questions that every GRE math section will have. You should Ballpark whenever you see the word "approximately" in a question, whenever the answer choices are far apart in value, and whenever you start to answer a question and you justifiably say to yourself, "This is going to take a lot of calculation!"

To help you ballpark, here are a few percents and their fractional equivalents:

$1\% = \dfrac{1}{100}$	$60\% = \dfrac{3}{5}$
$10\% = \dfrac{1}{10}$	$66\dfrac{2}{3}\% = \dfrac{2}{3}$
$20\% = \dfrac{1}{5}$	$75\% = \dfrac{3}{4}$
$25\% = \dfrac{1}{4}$	$80\% = \dfrac{4}{5}$
$33\dfrac{1}{3}\% = \dfrac{1}{3}$	$100\% = \dfrac{1}{1}$
$40\% - \dfrac{2}{5}$	$200\% = \dfrac{2}{1}$
$50\% = \dfrac{1}{2}$	

If, on a chart question, you were asked to find 9.6 percent of 21.4, you could ballpark by using 10 percent as a "friendlier" percentage and 20 as a "friendlier" number. Ten percent of 20 is 2. That's all you need to do to answer most chart questions.

Try out Ballparking on a real chart. Keep in mind that while friends give you charts to display the information they want you to see and to make that information easier to understand, ETS constructs charts to *hide* the information you need to know and to make that information *hard* to understand. So read all titles and small print, to make sure you understand what the charts are conveying.

Nationwide survey of ice cream preferences in 1975 and in 1985, by flavor.

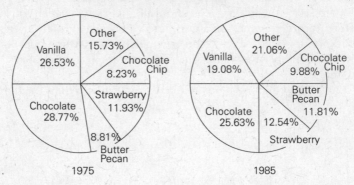

Looking over these charts, notice that they are for 1975 and 1985, and that all you know are percentages. There are no total numbers for the survey, and because the percentages are pretty "ugly," you can anticipate doing a lot of Ballparking to answer the questions. Try one:

To the nearest one percent, what percentage decrease in popularity occurred for chocolate from 1975 to 1985?

○　9%
○　10%
○　11%
○　89%
○　90%

First, we need to find the difference between 28.77 (the 1975 figure) and 25.63 (the 1985 figure). The difference is 3.14. Second, notice that ETS has asked for an approximate answer ("to the nearest one percent") which is screaming "Ballpark!" Could 3.14 really be 89 or 90 percent of 28.77? No way; it's closer to the neighborhood of 10 percent. Eliminate choices (D) and (E). Is it exactly 10 percent? No; that means choice B is out. Is it more or less than 10 percent? It's more—exactly 10 percent would be 2.877, and 3.14 is more than 2.877. That means the answer is (C).

Try another one:

> In 1985, if 20 percent of the "other" category is lemon flavor, and 4,212 people surveyed preferred lemon, then how many people were surveyed?
>
> ○   1,000
> ○   10,000
> ○   42,120
> ○   100,000
> ○ 1,000,000

The first piece of information you have is a percentage of a percentage. The percentage of people who preferred lemon in 1985 is equal to 20 percent of 21.06 percent. Make sure you see that before you go on. Now, notice that the numbers in the answer choices are very widely separated—they aren't consecutive integers. If you can just get in the ballpark, the answer will be obvious.

Rather than try to use 21.06 percent, we'll call it 20 percent. And rather than use 4,212, we'll use 4,000. The question is now: "20 percent of 20 percent of *what* is 4,000?" So, using translation, your equation looks like this:

$$\frac{20}{100} \times \frac{20}{100} \times x = 4,000$$

Do a little reducing.

$$\frac{1}{5} \times \frac{1}{5} \times x = 4,000$$

$$\frac{1}{25} \times x = 4,000$$

$$x = 100,000$$

That's (D).

GET ORGANIZED
WHEN DOING
ARITHMETIC

GET ORGANIZED WHEN DOING ARITHMETIC

Questions involving ratios or averages can seem daunting at first. The math involved in these problems, however, generally involves little more than basic arithmetic. The trick to these problems is understanding how to organize your information. Learning the triggers and set-ups for each of these problems can take a four-minute brain teaser and turn it into a 45-second cake walk.

Averages

Imagine you are asked to find the average of three numbers, 3, 7, and 8. This is not a difficult problem. Simply add the three together to get the total. Divide by three, the number of things, to get the average. All average problems involve three basic pieces:

- Total: 18

- # of things: 3

- Average: 6

It is virtually assured that they will never give you a list of numbers and ask you for the average. That would be too easy. They will, however, always give you two out of these three pieces, and it is your job to find the third. That's where the average pie comes in. The minute you see the word "average" on a problem, draw your pie on your scratch paper. It looks like this:

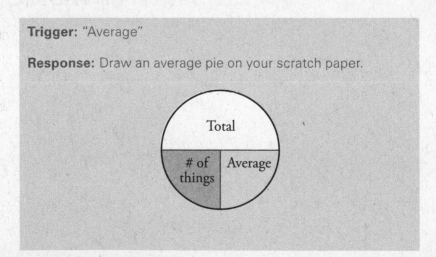

Trigger: "Average"

Response: Draw an average pie on your scratch paper.

Here's how you would fill it in.

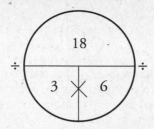

ETS won't necessarily give you a list of numbers and ask you to find the average. That would be too easy. They might give you the average and the total and ask you to find the number of things, or they might give you the number of things and the average and ask for the total. They will always give you two out of the three pieces of information. Just make your pie, fill in what you know, and it becomes easy to find the missing piece. Here's how it works:

The line in the middle means *divide*. If you have the total and the number of things, just divide and you get the average (18 ÷ 3 = 6). If you have the total and the average, just divide and you get the number of things (18 ÷ 6 = 3). If you have the average and the number of things, simply multiply and you get the total (6 × 3 = 18). As you will see, the key to most average questions is finding the total.

The benefit of the Average Pie is that you simply have to plug the information from the question into the Average Pie and then complete the Pie. Doing so will automatically give you all the information you need to answer the question.

Let's try this one:

The average (arithmetic mean) of a set of 6 numbers is 28. If a certain number, *y*, is removed from the set, the average of the remaining numbers in the set is 24.

Quantity A	Quantity B
y	48

○ Quantity A is greater.
○ Quantity B is greater.
○ The two quantities are equal.
○ The relationship cannot be determined from the information given.

The minute you see the word "average," make your pie. If you see the word "average" a second time, make a second pie. Start with the first bite-sized piece, "The average of a set of 6 numbers is 28." Draw your pie and fill it in. With the average and the number of things you can calculate the total, like this:

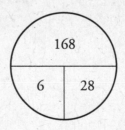

Take your next piece of the problem, "If a certain number, y, is removed from the set, the average of the remaining numbers in the set is 24." There's the word "average" again, so make another pie. Again, you have the number of things (5, because one number was removed from our set) and the average, 24, so you can calculate the total, like this:

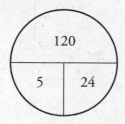

The total for all six numbers is 168. When you take a number out, the total for the remaining five is 120. The number you removed, therefore, must be $168 - 120 = 48$. $y = 48$. The answer is (C).

Ratios

When working with fraction, decimals, and percentages, you are working with a part to a whole relationship. The fraction $\frac{3}{5}$ means 3 parts out of a total of 5, and 20% means 20 parts out of every 100. A ratio on, the other hand, is a part to a part relationship. Lemons and limes in a ratio of 1 to 4 means that you have one lemon for every four limes. If you make an average pie every time you see the word "average," you should make a ratio box every time you see the word "ratio." Let's use an actual GRE problem:

Question 3 of 20

In a club with 35 members, the ratio of men to women is 2 to 3 among the members. How many men belong to the club?

○ 2
○ 5
○ 7
○ 14
○ 21

The problem says, "the ratio of men to woman..." As soon as you see that, make your box. It should look like this:

Men	Women	Total
			Ratio
			Multiplier
			Actual Number

In the top line of the box, list the items that make up your ratio, in this case, men and women. The last column is always for the total. In the second row of the box, fill in your ratio of 2 to 3 under Men and Women, respectively. The total is five. This doesn't mean that there are actually two men and three women in the club. This just means that for every five members of this club, two of them will be men and three of them will be women. The actual number of members, we're told in the problem, is 35. This goes in the bottom right cell under Total. With this single number in the bottom row we can figure out the rest. To get from 5 to 35, you need to multiply by 7. The multiplier remains constant across the ratio, so fill a 7 in all three cells of the third row, next to the word "multiplier." We now know that the actual number of men in the club is 14, just as the actual number of women is 21. Here's what your completed ratio box looks like:

	Men	Women	Total
Ratio	2 +	3 =	5
Multiply by	× 7 =	× 7 =	× 7 =
Actual Number	= 14	= 21	= 35

The fraction of the club that is male is $\frac{14}{35}$. If you reduce this, you get $\frac{2}{5}$. The percentage of members who are female is $\frac{3}{5}$ or 60%.

Median/Mode/Range

Median means the number in the middle, like the median strip on a highway. In the set of numbers 2, 2, 4, 5, 9, the median is "4" because it's the one in the middle. If the set had an even number of elements, let's say: 2, 3, 4, 6, the median is the average of the two numbers in the middle or, in this case, 3.5. That's it. There's not much that's interesting about the word "median." There are only two ways they can trick you with a median question. One is to give you a set with an even number of elements. We've mastered that one. The other is to give you a set of numbers which are out of order. If you see the word "median," therefore, find a bunch of numbers and put them in order.

"Mode" simply means the number that shows up the most. In the set 2, 2, 4, 5, 9, the mode is 2. That's all there is to mode. If no number shows up more than another, then the set has no mode.

"Range" is even easier. It is the difference between the biggest number in a set and the smallest. In other words, find the smallest number and subtract it from the biggest number.

Let's look at a problem:

Question 8 of 20

> If in the set of numbers {20, 14, 19, 12, 17, 20, 24}, v equals the mean, w equals the median, x equals the mode, and y equals the range, which of the following is true?
>
> ○ $v < w < x < y$
> ○ $v < x < w < y$
> ○ $y < v < w < x$
> ○ $y < v < x < w$
> ○ $w < y < v < x$

In this question we're asked to find the mean, the median, the mode, and the range of a set of numbers. The minute you see the word "median," you know what to do. Put the numbers in order: 12, 14, 17, 19, 20, 20, 24. Do this on your scratch paper, not in your head, and while you're at it, list A, B, C, D, and E so that you have something to eliminate. The minute we put the numbers in order, three out of the four elements we are asked to find become clear. The range, 12, is equal to the smallest number, so y should be the element at the far left of our series. Cross off A, B, and E. The average will be somewhere in the middle. Without doing some calculations, it's not clear if it is larger than the median (19) or smaller, so skip to the mode. The mode is 20 and larger than the median and certainly larger than the average. x should be the last element in our series. Cross off choice (D). The correct answer is (C). Always remember that the answer choices are part of the question. Often it is far easier to find and eliminate wrong answers than it is to find the right ones.

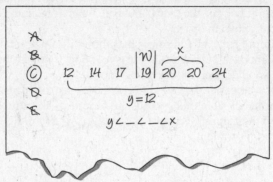

Rates and Proportions

Rates are really just proportions. Just like ratios and averages, the basic math is straight forward, but the difficult part is organizing the information. Actually, organizing the information is the whole trick. Set up all rates like a proportion and make sure you label the top and bottom of your proportion.

Let's look at an actual problem:

> Stan drives at an average speed of 60 miles per hour from Town A to Town B, a distance of 150 miles. Ollie drives at an average speed of 50 miles per hour from Town C to Town B, a distance of 120 miles.

Quantity A	Quantity B
Amount of time Stan spends driving	Amount of time Ollie spends driving

- ○ Quantity A is greater.
- ○ Quantity B is greater.
- ○ The two quantities are equal.
- ○ The relationship cannot be determined from the information given.

In this problem we are comparing two separate rates and each rate consists of miles (distance) and hours (time). Start with Stan. Stan's speed is 60 mph, which is to say that he drives 60 miles every one hour. We're asked to find how many hours it will take him to travel 150 miles. Just set it up as a proportion, like this:

$$\frac{miles}{hours} \quad \overset{Stan}{\frac{60}{1}} = \frac{150}{x} \quad \overset{Ollie}{\frac{50}{1}} = \frac{120}{x}$$

Now we can compare miles to miles and hours to hours. There is an x in the second space for hours because we don't yet know how many hours it's going to take Stan. The nice thing about this set-up is that you can always cross multiply to find the missing piece. If $60x = 150$, then $x = 2.5$. This means that it took Stan 2.5 hours to drive 150 miles (at a rate of 60 miles per hour).

Now try Ollie. The set up is the same. Ollie drives 50 miles for every one hour. To find out how many hours he needs to drive 120 miles, just cross multiply. If $50x = 120$, then $x = 2.4$. This means that it took Ollie 2.4 hours to drive 120 miles (at a rate of 50 miles per hour). Quantity A is Stan, so the correct answer is (A).

Arithmetic Summary

Trigger: When you see the word...   **Response:**

Trigger	Response
"Average"	Draw an Average Pie.
"Ratio"	Draw a ratio box.
"Median"	Find a bunch of numbers, and put them in order.
"Mode"	Find the number that appears the most often
"Range"	Subtract the smallest from the biggest.
"Rate"	Set up a proportion; label top and bottom.

PLAN BEFORE WRITING YOUR ESSAYS

PLAN BEFORE WRITING YOUR ESSAYS

The Issue Essay

Your issue essay will be read by two readers. At least one of them will be human. Yes, it's true. One of your readers will be a computer. ETS has developed a program that assesses the sophistication of the writing on student essays.

No matter who your readers are, they will be judging your essays on three basic criteria: the quality of your thinking, the quality of your organizing, and the quality of your writing. Essays are scored on a 1 to 6 scale in half-point increments. The two readers' scores will be averaged, and the two essay scores will be averaged. Quarter points are rounded up in the student's favor.

An essay with well-chosen examples, clear organization, and decent use of standard written English is automatically in the top half, guaranteeing you score of at least a 4. If any one of those categories is particularly strong, then your score goes from a 4 to a 5. If two of them are particularly strong, your score goes up to a 6. On the other hand, if any one of those three elements is missing, no matter what's going on with the other two, you are automatically in the bottom half. Since they will be judging your essays based upon these three criteria, we need a process that gives each its due.

You will be given two topics of general interest, from which you must select one. The topics will be of general enough interest that they are accessible to any test taker anywhere. ETS could never ask a question about, say, Hamlet, because this would advantage one group of test takers over another. Topics, therefore, tend to be about loss, growth, education, the role of government, individuals and society, and so on. In fact, all topics you might see are posted right now on www.GRE.org. The clock starts running the minute you see your topics, so pick one and get moving. It doesn't matter which one you pick; one is as good as the other.

Your job is to formulate an opinion about this topic and craft as convincing an argument as you can in support of your point of view. You will need to support your argument with specific examples. You can do anything you like with the issue topic (agree, disagree, even modify) as long as you stay on topic.

STEP 1: THINK

One of the most common mistakes that students make is that they write their essays based upon the first two or three examples they come up with. Rarely are these the best, or even the most interesting examples. Rarely do they show any development, and often they are the same examples that everyone else comes up with. ETS is judging you on the quality of your thinking, so take time to think.

Define the Topic

Topics come in three general flavors. There are extreme statements, wishy-washy statements, and open-ended statements. Your first job is to figure out what it means to agree or disagree with the statement. To agree with an extreme statement is to take an extreme position. This has the benefit of a very clear thesis statement, but may be difficult to defend. It is often easier to disagree with an extreme statement. To agree with a wishy-washy statement is usually pretty easy. Just say, "Sure, this is often true. Here are some examples…." To disagree with a wishy-washy statement is to take an extreme position. You must show that the statement is never true or always true. It is often easier to agree with a wishy-washy statement.

Brainstorm

Once you have defined the topic (this should take a minute or less), it's time to brainstorm. Your job, at this stage, is to push your thinking as far as it can go. Your job, whether you agree with the topic or not, is to come up with at least four "agree" examples, and four "disagree" examples. Quantity and variety are more important than quality at this point. On your scratch paper, draw a "T". on the left, write, "agree," and on the right write "disagree."

Your scratch paper should look like this:

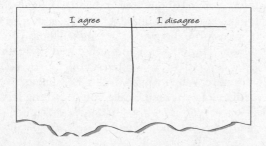

Argue From a Position of Strength

Topics are always general enough that they are accessible to all test takers, no matter who they are or where they're taking the test. This means that you can apply them to just about any area of expertise or experience. The place to start is with your own areas of expertise. How is the topic true for you? Could it apply to your field of study? Could it apply to your school? Is it true for your company? Go into the exam prepared to talk about the things you know best. What was your major in school? Where do you work now? What books have you recently read or papers have you have recently written? Essays written from an area of strength are always easier to write and far more convincing. It's always easier to talk about things you know well, and when you do, you will come across as an expert, because you are.

When your brainstorm runs dry, use this checklist:

> me, friends, family, school, city, country, company, species, old/young, history, science, literature

This should push your thinking in new directions. How is the topic true for the very old or the very young? What about at the species level? Could it occur in another species? Can it be true for an individual but also a country or company?

The first three examples you come up with are likely to be very similar. They might be three major figures in history, for example. One of those examples might be good, but the second and third don't advance your argument. Write them down as part of your brainstorm, but make sure to push your thinking into other areas. Each example you choose should have a specific job to do. They are the legs of the argument you are creating. An essay that shows development, or quality thinking, will look at the topic from multiple angles. Each example will bring something new to the argument.

Many students are worried about time at this stage. First, you are being judged on the quality of your thinking, so you cannot ignore this step. Next, a good brainstorm and a good outline will help you to be more efficient and more focused when you write. And lastly, thinking while you write is dangerous. Essays written on the fly often have a lack of focus and structure. When you are trying to think and work at the same time, you distract your brain while you're writing leading to embarrassing mistakes in grammar, punctuation, and diction.

The other thing to keep in mind is that ETS says specifically, "You are free to accept, reject, or qualify the claim made in the topic, as long as the ideas you present are clearly relevant to the topic you select." This means that you are free to approach the topic from any angle you want. It also means that you can focus on one particular area or application of the topic.

STEP 2: ORGANIZE

Most students come up with a point of view and then wrack their brains for the perfect examples to support it. They will often come up with that perfect example, but sometimes it doesn't happen until hours after the exam. The best way to have a perfect connection between your examples and your thesis statement is to select your examples first.

Some essay instructions will be relatively straight forward, such as "Present a point of view and support it with well-chosen examples." Other instructions may be more specific, such as "Present your position on the issue and describe a situation in which the implementation of your recommendation would not be advantageous." Paying close attention to the instructions you have been given, craft your point of view by selecting your three strongest examples. Be sure that each of your examples performs a specific and distinct job in support of your position.

Once you have selected your best examples, write a thesis statement to accommodate your examples. In this way, you will always have the perfect examples for your thesis statement because the examples came first! On your scratch paper, jot down your thesis, and underneath it, list your three examples in the order in which you plan to use them. Next to each example, jot down just a few words to remind yourself why you've chosen that example. This is the job that each example will perform in your argument, or why the example is a perfect illustration of your thesis.

You now have three interesting examples showing different perspectives on the issue: a thesis statement, which is perfectly supported by your examples; a clear, well organized outline for your essay; and even the makings of a topic sentence for each of your supporting paragraphs. Not only are you now ready to write, but when it comes time to write, you can focus just on your writing. You don't have to distract yourself from your writing by thinking about where your essay is going next. You've got a good clear plan. Stick to it. Your essay, at this point is 60% written. You have the majority of your intro paragraph and the beginning of the topic sentences for each of your supporting paragraphs. All you need to do is explain each of your examples in greater detail, come up with a conclusion, and you're done. It's time to start writing.

STEP 3: WRITE

When it comes to writing, there are two things your essay must have and a handful of things it could have to get credit for good writing.

Must Have:

1. **Topic sentences**—A topic sentence announces the subject and or point of each supporting paragraph. It could be quite literal such as "_____ is an example of why _[restate your thesis]_," or something more nuanced. Use your topic sentence to link each example to your thesis and to indicate to the reader the point you would like each example to make. Make it easy for your reader to get your point and the direction in which you are going. The harder your reader has to work to find your point, the lower your score will go. It does not pay to be overly subtle when your reader will spend only one to two minutes on your essay.

2. **Transitions**—Transitions give your essay flow. They indicate changes in scale, direction, or perspective, and help the reader get from one paragraph to the next. It might be just a few words attached to your topic sentence or a whole sentence. If you are changing direction, for example, simply saying "on the other hand" or "in contrast" might be sufficient. If you are changing scale or perspective, you might say "when viewed from the perspective of a ___" or "What is true for an individual is equally true for a ____. For example..."

Might Have:

1. **Specifics**—When you argue from a position of strength, these should be easy. Use names, dates, places, and any other relevant details. The details bring an example to life and make you sound like an expert.

2. **Quotes**—In many ways, a quote is like the ultimate specific. You can't always use quotes, but if you have a good one and you can drop it comfortably into your essay, it's quite impressive.

3. **Big Words**—Big words used correctly always score points. They are a way to distinguish yourself from the other writers. They are also something that can be prepared in advance. Generate a list of impressive words that you know well and look for places to use them.

4. **Analogies**—To say that censorship, for example, is a double-edged sword may be a bit clichéd, but it is also a terrific way to set up an argument that has two sides. Using a good metaphor is like tucking a snazzy silk handkerchief in your breast pocket. It's not necessary, or even common, but if you can pull it off, it raises the whole ensemble to another level.

5. **Length**—Length counts. Statistically speaking, longer essays score better. That means beefing up your typing skills. If you have time, drop in a fourth example or add a few more details to each of your first three examples.

6. **Rhetorical questions**—Does anything sound more professorial in an essay than the occasional rhetorical question? It is a rhetorical flourish that is rarely used but particularly effective for this type of essay. It allows you to speak directly to your reader and represents a sophisticated way of jumping into a topic that most writers never consider.

7. **Commands**—Use them. They will grab the reader's attention. It is a bold style of writing that few people use.

THE ARGUMENT ESSAY

Analysis of an Argument

On the issue essay, your job is to craft your own argument. On the argument essay, your job is the opposite. You will be given someone else's argument, and you must break it down and assess it. In some ways, this is not difficult. The argument you're given will be filled with some pretty obvious flaws.

Here's an example of the type of prompts you will see for your argument essay:

The following appeared in a memorandum from the regional manager of the Taste of Italy restaurant chain.

"After the first month of service, the new restaurant in the Flatplains Mall, which uses the Chipless brand of wine glasses, has reported a far lower rate of breakage than our other restaurants that use the Elegance brand. Since servers and a bartenders at all of our restaurants frequently report that breakage is a result of the type of wineglass, and the customers at the Flatplains Mall restaurant seem to like the Chipless style of glasses, we should switch all of our restaurants over to the Chipless brand."

Instructions

The argument text will be followed by a brief series of instructions. You may be asked for ways to strengthen an argument, find alternative explanations for an argument (weaken), discuss questions to be asked about the argument (identify premise and assumptions), discuss evidence needed to evaluate the argument, and so on. All instructions will ask you to work with the basic parts of an argument in some way. No matter what, you must be prepared to identify the parts of an argument, different types of argument, and how they all work.

Breaking down the Argument

There are three basic parts to any argument.

The Conclusion
The conclusion is the point of the argument. The author is trying to convince you of something. That something is the conclusion. Typically, the conclusion will be stated, and it is often indicated by words such as "therefore" or "in conclusion." It is possible, however, for a conclusion to be implied.

The Premises
Once you identify the conclusion, ask yourself, "Why?" The answers to that question that are stated in the argument are the premises. They are always stated. There will be a few of them. They are the evidence cited to support the conclusion.

Assumptions
Assumptions are never stated. They link the conclusion to the premises, and there are hundreds of assumptions. When you brainstorm an argument, it is assumptions you are looking for. They are all of the things that have to be true in order for the conclusion to be true.

When you begin to break down an argument, you will want to use the formal language of arguments. First, identify the conclusion, then the premises, and finally the assumptions.

Types of Arguments

There are some types of arguments that you will see frequently. Once you identify the type of argument being made, spotting the assumption is easy.

Causal: A Causes B

A causal argument assumes a cause-and-effect relationship between two events. *For example, employee turnover is up because salaries are down.* The conclusion is that lower salaries caused employee turnover to go up. To weaken a causal argument, you need to point out other potential causes for a particular event. Perhaps employee turnover is up because of a change in management or other policies. Perhaps there is another company offering better jobs. To strengthen a causal argument, you need to show that other potential causes are unlikely.

Sampling or Statistical: A = A, B, C

In these arguments the author assumes that a particular group represents an entire population. For example, *nine out of ten doctors surveyed prefer a particular brand of chewing gum.* The conclusion is that 90% of all doctors prefer this brand of chewing gum. Is that true? To weaken this argument, you need to show that the people in the group surveyed don't represent the whole population. Perhaps they surveyed doctors at the chewing gums annual shareholder meeting. Perhaps they surveyed doctors in the city where the chewing gum has its headquarters. To strengthen this argument, you need to show that the sample population is, in fact, representative of the whole.

Analogy: A = B

Analogy arguments claim that what is true for one group is also true for another. For example, *football players like a particular brand of cleats, so soccer players should too.* The conclusion is that soccer players should like this brand of cleats. Why? Because football players like them. This is the premise. The main assumption is that soccer players should like the same thing as football players. Is this true? To weaken analogy arguments you need to show that the two groups are not at all analogous. Perhaps football players prefer cleats that offer foot protection while soccer players want ones that mold to the foot. To strengthen these arguments, you must show that the two groups are quite similar indeed (at least in their shoe choice).

Crafting Your Argument Essay

The overall process for crafting your essay will be the same as it is for the issue essay. Invariably, you will have to follow the approach dictated by your instructions. Although, no matter what you will need to identify and address weaknesses in the argument. Throughout your essay you want to use the language of arguments. That means naming conclusions as conclusions, sampling arguments as sampling arguments, premises as premises, and assumptions as assumptions.

Thinking

Begin by identifying your conclusion and then identify the major premises upon which it rests. For each premise note the type of reasoning used (sampling, casual, and so on), and the flaws associated with that type of reasoning. This is as much brainstorming as you will need.

Organizing

Rank the premises by the size of their flaws. Start with the most egregious and work your way down. The outline of your essay will look something like this:

- The author's conclusion is z. It is faulty and more research/information is needed before the suggested action is taken.

- The first and biggest flaw is premise y. It's possible that it is true, but it rests upon the following assumptions. Can we really make these assumptions? What about these alternative assumptions?

- Even if we assume y to be the case, there is premise x. Premise x draws an analogy between these two groups and assumes that they are interchangeable. Can we really make this assumption? What about these alternative assumptions?

- Even if we assume x to be true, there is also w. W is a sampling argument, but the author not only has not proven the sample to be representative, but he/she also points out that this may not be the case! Perhaps, as noted, blah, blah, blah.

In conclusion, this argument is incomplete and rests upon too many questionable assumptions. To improve this argument, the author needs to show *a, b,* and *c,* before the building is to be torn down (or the company is to change tactics or the school is to reorganize its curriculum, insert argument conclusion here).

Writing

Feel free to have fun with this essay. Reading essays can get pretty boring, and a smart, funny critique of a faulty argument can be a welcomed break for your reader. You might say, "If I were the president of company *x,* I would fire my marketing director for wasting my time with such a poorly researched plan." It is OK to have personality as long as you get the analysis of the argument done at the same time.

For a more in-depth look at the techniques for the argument essay and some sample essays, see our *Cracking the New GRE* book.

PART **III**

DRILLS

VERBAL DRILL #1

1. Children, after more than a generation of television, have become "hasty viewers"; as a result, if the camera lags, the attention of these young viewers _____.

   ○ expands
   ○ starts
   ○ alternates
   ○ wanes
   ○ clarifies

2. Certainly the architect's _____ is not due to his promotional skills, indeed, he isolated himself from everything that could disturb his work.

   ○ proficiency
   ○ temperament
   ○ prominence
   ○ superiority
   ○ reticence

3. The violinist's (i) _____ performance, coupled with the (ii) _____ cadences of the renowned composer's music, roused the audience to a standing ovation.

Blank (i)	Blank (ii)
prosaic	soporific
hackneyed	mellifluous
virtuosic	insipid

4. Research into early childhood education, which advocates providing toddlers as young as two or three with a plenitude of intellectually-stimulating activities, has produced (i) _____ results. Such findings, however, have failed to (ii) _____ many parents from enrolling their children in such unproven programs.

Blank (i)	Blank (ii)
conclusive	disabuse
ambiguous	dissuade
auspicious	distinguish

5. Classical economics views humans as rational, pragmatic creatures who nonetheless seek to maximize their own (i) _____. Veblen, in contrast, depicts humans as (ii) _____ beings, pursuing social status with (iii) _____ regard for their own happiness.

Blank (i)	Blank (ii)	Blank (iii)
melancholy	irrational	sporadic
bliss	pugnacious	scant
discord	mundane	stoic

6. While (i) _____ has always been a problem in college classrooms, some feared the availability of online resources would cause the problem to (ii) _____. However, educators have been able to take advantage of internet tools to check their students' work against any material online and thus (iii) _____ that their students are truly submitting their own work and not simply copying from a website.

Blank (i)	Blank (ii)	Blank (iii)
tardiness	proliferate	ensure
abstraction	descend	rebut
plagiarism	delineate	neglect

7. The skill level of medieval stoneworkers clearly exceeds that of their modern counterparts. A trade journal recently published the results of a decade-long survey of master stonemasons in Europe. According to the report, a clear majority of respondents noted that medieval cathedrals exhibit a consistently higher level of craftsmanship in their stonework than do similar edifices built in the last hundred years.

Which of the following, if true, would most seriously weaken the above argument?

○ The stonemason's main tools are virtually unchanged since the Middle Ages.

○ The stonework in cathedrals is typical of that in surviving medieval structures.

○ Most medieval cathedrals are significantly larger than modern stone edifices.

○ The practice of apprenticeship had declined significantly since the Middle Ages.

○ Higher quality stonework is less likely to fall into disrepair and be destroyed.

Reading Comprehension

Questions 8–11 refer to the following passage.

Although the study of women's history has only been developed as an academic discipline in the last twenty years, it is not the case that the current wave of feminist activity is the first in which interest in women's past was manifest.
5 From its very beginnings, the nineteenth-century English women's movement sought to expand existing knowledge of the activities and achievements of women in the past. At the same time, like its American counterpart, the English women's movement had a powerful sense of its own his-
10 toric importance and of its relationship to wider social and political change.

Nowhere is this sense of the historical importance—and of the historical connections between the women's move-
15 ment and other social and political developments—more evident than in Ray Strachey's classic account of the movement, *The Cause.* "The true history of the Women's Movement," Strachey argues, "is the whole history of the nineteenth century." The women's movement was part of
20 the broad sweep of liberal and progressive reform that was transforming society. Strachey emphasized this connection between the women's movement and the broader sweep of history by highlighting the influence of the Enlightenment and the Industrial Revolution on it. The protest made by
25 the women's movement at the confinement and injustices faced by women was, in Strachey's view, part of the liberal attack on traditional prejudices and injustice. This critique of women's confinement was supplemented by the demand for recognition of women's roles in the public, particularly
30 the philanthropic realm. Indeed, it was the criticism of the limitations faced by women on the one hand, and their establishment of a new public role on the other hand, that provided the core of the movement, determining also its form: its organization around campaigns for legal, political,
35 and social reform.

Strachey's analysis was a very illuminating one, nowhere
more so than in her insistence that, despite their differences and even antipathy to each other, both the radical
Mary Wollstonecraft and evangelical Hannah More need
40 to be seen as forerunners of mid-Victorian feminism. At
the same time, she omitted some issues that now seem
crucial to any discussion of the context of Victorian feminism. Where Strachey pictured a relatively fixed image
of domestic women throughout the first half of the nine-
45 teenth century, recent historical and literary works suggest that this image was both complex and unstable. The
establishment of a separate domestic sphere for women
was but one aspect of the enormous change in sexual
and familial relationships that was occurring from the late
50 eighteenth through the mid-nineteenth century. These
changes were accompanied by both anxiety and uncer-
tainty and by the constant articulation of women's duties
in a new social world.

8. The primary purpose of the passage is to
   ○ present an overview of the economic changes
     that led to the English
     women's movement
   ○ evaluate a view of the English women's movement
     as presented in a literary work
   ○ describe the social and political context of the
     women's movement in England
   ○ offer a novel analysis of England's reaction to
     the women's movement
   ○ profile several of the women who were instru-
     mental in the success of the English women's
     movement

9. The author includes Strachey's claim that "the true history of the Women's Movement . . . is the whole history of the nineteenth century" (lines 17–19) in order to emphasize

○ Strachey's belief that the advancement of women's rights was the most significant development of its century

○ the importance Strachey attributes to the women's movement in bringing about the Enlightenment

○ Strachey's awareness of the interconnection of the women's movement and other societal changes in the 1800s

○ Strachey's contention that the women's movement, unlike other social and political developments of the time, actually transformed society

○ Strachey's argument that the nineteenth century must play a role in any criticism of the limitations of women

10. While the author acknowledges Strachey's importance in the study of women's history, she faults Strachey for

○ focusing her study on the legal and political reform enacted by the women's movement

○ oversimplifying her conception of the social condition of women prior to the reforms of the women's movement

○ failing to eliminate the anachronistic idea of "women's duty" from her articulation of nineteenth-century feminism

○ omitting Mary Wollstonecraft and Hannah More from her discussion of important influences in feminism

○ recommending a static and domestic social role for women following the women's movement

11. Which of the following, if true, would most weaken the author's assertion about the similarity between the English and American women's movements?

○ The English and American women's movements took place in very different sociohistorical climates.

○ The English women's movement began almost a century before the American women's movement.

○ The English women's movement excluded men, while the American women's movement did not.

○ Few members of the English women's movement were aware of the impact it would have on society.

○ Many participants in the English women's movement continued to perform traditional domestic roles.

12. Though not completely _____, the newest edition of the book is certainly very different from any previously published version.

☐ familiar

☐ unrecognizable

☐ answerable

☐ legitimate

☐ reworked

☐ gentrified

13. Merzon's _____ behavior convinced his colleagues that he had ulterior motives.

☐ inconspicuous

☐ furtive

☐ overt

☐ unorthodox

☐ predictable

☐ surreptitious

14. With its refined interiors and amply stocked reading room, the hotel catered to the most _____ of travelers.

☐ philistine

☐ urbane

☐ cosmopolitan

☐ uncouth

☐ grandiloquent

☐ pretentious

15. By far not the most _____ of men, Wilbert nonetheless enjoyed renown that was unimpeded by his inherent irascibility.

☐ loquacious

☐ pedantic

☐ amiable

☐ garrulous

☐ affable

☐ stentorian

16. Click on the sentence in the passage that best supports the author's main idea.

It is hard from our modern perspective to imagine that theater has the power to influence politics, yet the plays of prerepublican Ireland did just that. Crippled by the censorious English rule and muted by population migration, Irish culture had fallen into an almost irrevocable decline by the second half of the 19th Century. A group of Dublin intellectuals and writers, calling themselves the Gaelic League, formed a society dedicated to the revival of Irish culture. Among its illustrious members, the League boasted William Butler Yeats, J.M. Synge, Sean O'Casey, and Lady Gregory. The founding of the Abbey Theatre and the production of Irish plays were directly responsible for the resurgence of interest in Irish language and culture, culminating in the European Union's decision in 2005 to make Irish an official language of that body.

Questions 17–20 refer to the following passage.

Following the discovery in 1895 that malaria is carried by *Anopheles* mosquitoes, governments around the world set out to eradicate those insect vectors. In Europe, the relation between the malarial agent, protozoan blood parasites of
5   the genus Plasmodium, and the vector mosquito, *Anopheles maculipennis,* seemed at first inconsistent. In some localities the mosquito was abundant but malaria rare or absent, while in others the reverse was true. In 1934 the problem was solved. Entomologists discovered that *A. maculipennis* is not
10 a single species but a group of at least seven.

In outward appearance, the adult mosquitoes seem almost identical, but in fact they are marked by a host of distinctive biological traits, some of which prevent them from hybrid-
15 izing. Some of the species distinguished by these traits were found to feed on human blood and thus to carry the malarial parasites. Once identified, the dangerous members of the *A. maculipennis* complex could be targeted and eradicated.

17. Which of the following best describes the reason that scientists were initially perplexed at the discovery that malaria was spread by *Anopheles* mosquitoes?

○ Scientists had evidence that malaria was carried by the protozoan blood parasite Plasmodium.

○ Scientists felt that because so many species of *Anopheles* existed, they could not be carriers.

○ Scientists were unable to find a direct correla-tion between *Anopheles* density and frequency of malaria occurrence.

○ Scientists knew that many species of *Anopheles* mosquito did not feed on human blood.

○ Scientists believed that the *Anopheles* mosquito could not be host to the parasite Plasmodium.

18. In the context in which it appears, "host" (line 13) most nearly means
    ○ scarcity
    ○ sacrament
    ○ multitude
    ○ organism receiving a transplant
    ○ organism supporting a parasite

19. It can be inferred from the passage that a mosquito becomes a carrier of malaria when
    ○ it ingests the blood of a human being infected with malaria
    ○ it lives in regions where malaria is widespread
    ○ it consumes blood from a protozoan malarial agent
    ○ it has extended contact with other insect vectors
    ○ it is spawned in Plasmodium-infested localities

20. The bolded text plays which of the following roles in the passage?
    ○ It provides evidence to weaken the author's main point.
    ○ It provides evidence to strengthen the author's main point.
    ○ It clarifies the importance of solving a paradox expressed in the passage.
    ○ It gives the resolution to a paradox expressed in the passage.
    ○ It explains why a paradox expressed in the passage resisted easy resolution.

VERBAL DRILL 2

1. Many scholars feel that historical events can be seen as _____; what one group sees as peace-keeping, another group might see as subjugation.
   - ○ academic
   - ○ portentous
   - ○ paradoxical
   - ○ trifling
   - ○ bellicose

2. The American public venerates medical researchers because the researchers make frequent discoveries of tremendous humanitarian consequence; however, the daily routines of scientists are largely made up of result verification and statistical analysis, making their occupation seem _____.
   - ○ fascinating
   - ○ quotidian
   - ○ recalcitrant
   - ○ experimental
   - ○ amorphous

3. The (i) _____ clothing store faced its first real crisis just six months after opening when new owners took over the building, raised the rent (ii) _____, and asked for a five-year extension on the lease.

Blank (i)	Blank (ii)
fledgling	beneficently
urbane	precipitously
ostentatious	minutely

4. Ronald Reagan became known as "The Great Communicator" particularly because of his ability to make (i) _____ topics in domestic and foreign affairs more (ii) _____ to persons of widely varying educational levels.

Blank (i)	Blank (ii)
abstruse	palatable
obtuse	lucid
mundane	munificent

5. The census taker's (i) _____ job is made even more difficult by the (ii) _____ nature of modern civilization. Increasing numbers of people seldom reside in any one place for very long. Even among those who do remain (iii) _____, however, there are frequent changes of livelihood, income, and even socioeconomic status.

Blank (i)	Blank (ii)	Blank (iii)
arduous	inert	itinerant
facile	transient	contrite
facetious	aesthetic	static

6. By nightfall the city council debate had long since degenerated into (i) _____. What had begun in the late afternoon as an earnest but polite discussion turned personal as both sides hurled (ii) _____ and personal attacks at each other. Disinterested observers, however, blamed the (iii) _____ chairman of the council for allowing such disarray, arguing that a moderator with more experience could have managed the meeting more constructively.

Blank (i)	Blank (ii)	Blank (iii)
complacency	acclamations	neophyte
parity	perturbations	assiduous
bedlam	epithets	exuberant

Reading Comprehension

Questions 7–9 refer to the following passage.

One popular but controversial way of regaining revenue shortfalls in professional sports is to sell stadium naming rights. Building a new sports or entertainment facility is a major financial undertaking; as branding and sponsorship
5 become increasingly ubiquitous, it is perhaps inevitable that big business will shoulder more of the burden in exchange for publicity.

Theoretically, the selling of naming rights seems like a
10 win-win proposition, but practically, the situation is more complicated. Fans are often opposed to changing the name of a stadium, or want to make sure their contribution to its construction is recognized. Neighborhood residents may also object to a perceived redecoration of their community
15 in corporate colors, logos and advertisements. For companies, naming rights alone often do not justify the high prices charged. Additionally, it is unclear whether the team or the facility benefits from the sale: if the corporation is a "sponsor," the team should receive the money, but facility
20 owners glean revenue from "advertisers." Thus, the difficulty of reaching a mutually acceptable wording of complicated agreements creates a quagmire of litigation.

Several means of compromise have been negotiated, such as selling the name of the field while keeping the original
25 name of the sports arena, selling sections of the facility, allowing a company to "present" it, allowing the sponsor to provide retail or concession services inside the stadium, and offering business opportunities such as direct-to-consumer coupons, product samples, and information. Though the
30 practice was nearly unheard of thirty-five years ago, there are currently 72 sponsorship deals in place. And sports is not the only area to "go corporate"—convention centers, concert venues, public works, and even educational institutions have sold naming rights in exchange for much-needed funds and
35 services.

7. The passage mentions the difference between "sponsors" and "advertisers" primarily in order to

- ○ illustrate the confusing nature of legal proceedings that surround naming rights' deals
- ○ provide an example of the kinds of issues that surround a naming rights agreement
- ○ prove that it is always important to consider terminology carefully
- ○ reveal the pernicious nature of one and the benevolent nature of the other
- ○ explain why communities often do not benefit from neighborhood stadiums

8. In which sentence of the passage does the author attempt to anticipate and preclude a possible reaction on the part of the reader?

○ Building a new sports or entertainment facility is a major financial undertaking; as branding and sponsorship become increasingly ubiquitous, it is perhaps inevitable that big business will shoulder more of the burden in exchange for publicity.

○ Theoretically, the selling of naming rights seems like a win-win proposition, but practically, the situation is more complicated.

○ For companies, naming rights alone often do not justify the high prices charged.

○ Thus, the difficulty of reaching a mutually acceptable wording of complicated agreements creates a quagmire of litigation.

○ Though the practice was nearly unheard of thirty-five years ago, there are currently 72 sponsorship deals in place.

9. In the context in which it appears in the last paragraph, the word "practice" most nearly means

○ observance
○ rite
○ rehearsal
○ action
○ office

Questions 10–11 refer to the following passage.

Often lost in the uproariously ribald nature of Aristophanes' great wartime comedy Lysistrata (411 BCE) is the author's serious message. Contemporary audiences, like modern ones, were taken by the story of Lysistrata organizing the
5 Greek women to withhold sexual favors until peace is declared between Athens and Sparta. To its Athenian audience, though, embroiled in seemingly endless Peloponnesian War, the work had a clear symbolic meaning: end the war,

but through celebration of Greek unity, not celibacy. The part
10 meant to resonate with viewers was not the withholding of
sex, but the power of the concord the women showed in so
doing. The play's women, in fact, represent the Greek poleis,
or city-states. The protagonists, Lysistrata and Lampito, represent Athens and Sparta, respectively; the conspiracy can't
15 begin until Lampito arrives, and peace can be achieved only
when they make common cause with the other women. The
women's cohesion carries them through their confrontation
with the magistrate and his henchmen, and is emphasized in
the oracle: the ills of life will end when "the swallows...shall
20 have all flocked together." And the men only finally agree to
give the women a hearing when they realize that they're fac-
ing "a general conspiracy embracing all Greece." The men,
for their part, represent anti-Greek, polis-based attitudes, and
are only overcome when led by Lysistrata to focus on Greek
25 commonalities, instances of past mutual aid, and the shared
external threat of the Persians.

10. With which of the following statements would the
author most likely agree?
- ○ Aristophanes was uniquely influential among
Athenian playwrights.
- ○ Wartime comedies without a serious message
are inappropriate subjects of study.
- ○ Some knowledge of history can be useful in
interpreting literature from other eras.

11. The author mentions the oracle primarily in order to
- ○ emphasize the importance of Lampito among
the conspirators
- ○ provide additional evidence in support of the
main idea of the passage
- ○ clarify the origins of the conspiracy in the play
- ○ suggest that earlier interpretations of Lysistrata
were based on false assumptions
- ○ concede a point in opposition to the main idea
of the passage

Question 12 refers to the following passage.

Statistics released by the National Institute of Health show that cancer patients, on average, are living almost six months longer after the initial diagnosis of their condition than were patients just two years ago. Moreover,
5   these findings conform to a trend that goes back well over a decade. Clearly, the medical community is making significant progress in extending the lives of cancer patients.

12. The above argument depends on which of the following as an assumption?
  ○ Cancer is not being diagnosed in progressively earlier stages.
  ○ The trend is more pronounced in some kinds of cancer than in others.
  ○ Fewer people are diagnosed with cancer each year.
  ○ The number of patients whose cancer goes into full remission is also rising.
  ○ Cancer is no longer the leading cause of death among people over 60 years of age.

13. Fervent schisms among the delegates were largely overplayed; the area of _____ was sizable enough to keep the convention from being disbanded.

  ☑ congruence
  ☐ asperity
  ☐ contradiction
  ☐ concurrence
  ☐ impassivity
  ☐ truculence

14. What Andrew Johnson lacked in education he made up for with his _____; though he never attended school, he taught himself to read and write, entered politics, and ultimately succeeded Abraham Lincoln as president of the United States.

- ☐ mettle
- ☐ timidity
- ☐ tenacity
- ☐ tenuousness
- ☐ candor
- ☐ alacrity

15. The _____ sales clerk, desperate to unload her burgeoning inventory, unwittingly drove many a potential customer away with her pushy, overeager manner.

- ☐ loquacious
- ☐ irreverent
- ☐ officious
- ☐ innocuous
- ☐ meddlesome
- ☐ vigilant

16. _____ is no guarantee of worker loyalty; even the most compliant of employees may be motivated by a hidden agenda.

- ☐ effrontery
- ☐ deference
- ☐ prevarication
- ☐ complaisance
- ☐ truculence
- ☐ chicanery

Questions 17–18 refer to the following passage.

Research conducted on the neurological consequences of illicit substances traditionally has centered on the blockage of the reuptake neurons (DAT) that, under normal conditions, recycle dopamine (DA) to prevent overstimulation. As seen
5 in the brain of a healthy, non substance-abusing individual, DA is released through an electric pulse, it lingers momentarily around dopamine receptors (D2) to pique the body, and then travels back up DAT for later use. Recently, positron emission tomography has enabled researchers to a discover
10 an unexpected, completely different process: drug use may actually decrease the quantity of D2 available to receive DA, resulting in a perceived deficit of the latter and an irrepressible compulsion, the hallmark of addiction, to increase its production through stimulants.

17. In the context in which is appears, "pique" most nearly means
   ○ impair
   ○ heal
   ○ excite
   ○ relax
   ○ irritate

18. The passage explains the conventional focus of substance abuse research in order to
   ○ argue that such an approach is based on a false understanding of the way that most illegal drugs act on the brain
   ○ suggest that the positron emission technology is not accurate in its depiction of D2 reduction
   ○ provide evidence in favor of continuing research into DAT blockage
   ○ make clear why the discovery of an alternate consequence of substance abuse might be unexpected
   ○ offer a reasonable explanation for the inability of many people to overcome drug addiction

Questions 19–20 refer to the following passage.

One of the most significant reasons for the dramatic rise in both agricultural production and population in western Europe around 1000 CE was the increase in the use of horses as draft animals. The military preeminence of
5   mounted cavalry since the Carolingian era meant that horses were selectively bred for size and strength earlier than were other farm animals, and the ninth-century development of nailed horseshoes improved both traction and resistance against infection. Most importantly,
10 perhaps, harnesses designed for oxen were adapted for horses: a neck strap that restricted both air and blood from reaching the horse's brain was reconfigured to put the weight on the horse's shoulders, and horses quickly shed their ancient stigma as lazy beasts.
15
The change from ox to horse as the primary draft animal was slow and erratic. **Horses were expensive, untraditional, and required an expensive food, oats.** Where the change occurred, though, it gave the European country-
20 side a new look by greatly increasing the amount of land that could be exploited from a central homestead. Where once farmers were limited to fields to which they could drive their oxen, plow, and return home in a day, they could now ride their horses much greater distances, do a
25 day's work, and still return to safety before dark. Isolated hamlets grew towards each other to form vast villages, which, in turn, expanded into towns, and the great primeval forests of Europe receded into memory.

19. The passage provides information to answer which of the following questions?
   ○ How far from a central homestead could oxen be driven for a day's work?
   ○ What developments helped lead to the military primacy of horses?
   ○ What made ancient harnesses unsuitable for horses?

20. In the above passage, the text in boldface plays which of the following roles?

○ It cites factors facilitating the development under discussion.

○ It cites factors inhibiting the development under discussion.

○ It eliminates an alternate cause for the development under discussion.

○ It resolves a paradox presented in the passage.

○ It suggests further ramifications of a paradox presented in the passage.

MATH DRILL 1

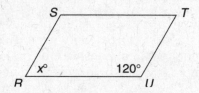

RSTU is a parallelogram

1.   Quantity A   Quantity B

                  x   45

○ Quantity A is greater.

○ Quantity B is greater.

○ The two quantities are equal.

○ The relationship cannot be determined from the information given.

Mr. Jones purchased a new bedroom set by using an extended payment plan. The regular price of the set was $900, but on the payment plan he paid $300 up front and 9 monthly payments of $69 each.

2.

Quantity A	Quantity B
$23	The amount Mr. Jones paid in addition to the regular price of the bedroom set.

○ Quantity A is greater.
○ Quantity B is greater.
○ The two quantities are equal.
○ The relationship cannot be determined from the information given.

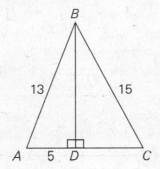

3.

Quantity A	Quantity B
The perimeter of triangle BCD	42

○ Quantity A is greater.
○ Quantity B is greater.
○ The two quantities are equal.
○ The relationship cannot be determined from the information given.

The circumference of a circle with a radius of $\frac{1}{2}$ meter is C meters.

4.

Quantity A	Quantity B
C	4

○ Quantity A is greater.
○ Quantity B is greater.
○ The two quantities are equal.
○ The relationship cannot be determined from the information given.

5.

Quantity A	Quantity B
$x + 1$	$1 - x$

○ Quantity A is greater.
○ Quantity B is greater.
○ The two quantities are equal.
○ The relationship cannot be determined from the information given.

The average (arithmetic mean) of two positive integers is equal to 17. Each of the integers is greater than 12.

6.

Quantity A	Quantity B
Twice the larger of the two integers	44

○ Quantity A is greater.
○ Quantity B is greater.
○ The two quantities are equal.
○ The relationship cannot be determined from the information given.

7.

Quantity A	Quantity B
xy	$x\sqrt{y}$

○ Quantity A is greater.
○ Quantity B is greater.
○ The two quantities are equal.
○ The relationship cannot be determined from the information given.

8.

Quantity A	Quantity B
30	The number of integers from 15 to −15, inclusive

○ Quantity A is greater.
○ Quantity B is greater.
○ The two quantities are equal.
○ The relationship cannot be determined from the information given.

9. Mike bought a used car and had it repainted. If the cost of the paint job was one-fifth of the purchase price of the car, and if the cost of the car and the paint job combined was $4,800, then what was the purchase price of the car?

○ $800
○ $960
○ $3,840
○ $4,000
○ $4,250

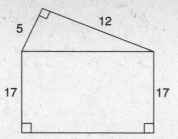

Note: Figure is not drawn to scale.

10. What is the perimeter of the figure above?
    ○ 51
    ○ 64
    ○ 68
    ○ 77
    ○ 91

11. If x and y are integers and xy is an even integer, which of the following must be an odd integer?
    ○ $xy + 5$
    ○ $x + y$
    ○ $\dfrac{x}{y}$
    ○ $4x$
    ○ $7xy$

12. If $3x = -2$, then $(3x - 3)^2 =$ ☐

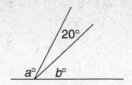

13. In the figure above, what does b equal if $a = 3b$?
    ○ 40
    ○ 30
    ○ 25
    ○ 20
    ○ 10

Questions 14–16 refer to the following chart.

REGISTERED VOTERS IN TOWNSHIP X IN 2010				
Distribution by Age and Gender			**Percent of Registered Voters by Political Affiliation**	
Age	**Male**	**Female**	**Affiliation**	**Percent**
18 to 32	1,030	1,104	Democrat	43%
33 to 47	1,114	1,259	Republican	41%
48 to 62	1,291	1,306	Other, including Independent	16%
63 and older	947	1,002		
Total	4,382	4,671		

14. If the total number of registered voters in Township X increased 10% from 2000 to 2010, then how many registered voters were in Township X in 2000 ?

[   ]

15. How many registered voters in Township X in 2010 were females, less than 48 years old, or both?
    ○ 5,701
    ○ 5,715
    ○ 6,745
    ○ 6,815
    ○ 8,106

16. In Township X in 2010, the ratio of the number of voters registered as Democrats to the number of male registered voters age 48 to 62 was most nearly
    ○ 1 to 1
    ○ 2 to 1
    ○ 3 to 1
    ○ 3 to 2
    ○ 5 to 2

17. What is the least number r for which $(3r + 2)(r - 3) = 0$?
    ○ –3
    ○ –2
    ○ $-\dfrac{2}{3}$
    ○ $\dfrac{2}{3}$
    ○ 3

18. What is the perimeter, in centimeters, of a rectangular newspaper ad 14 centimeters wide that has the same area as a rectangular newspaper ad 52 centimeters long and 28 centimeters wide?

    [   ]

19. In a certain election, 60 percent of the voters were women. If 30 percent of the women and 20 percent of the men voted for candidate X, what percent of all the voters in that election voted for candidate X?
   - ○ 18%
   - ○ 25%
   - ○ 26%
   - ○ 30%
   - ○ 50%

20. Which of the following is an integer if

   $K = 21 \times 54 \times 22$?

   - □ $\dfrac{K}{15}$
   - □ $\dfrac{K}{27}$
   - □ $\dfrac{K}{33}$
   - □ $\dfrac{K}{48}$
   - □ $\dfrac{K}{63}$
   - □ $\dfrac{K}{75}$

MATH DRILL 2

1.

Quantity A	Quantity B
$4(2^6)$	$6(4^2)$

○ Quantity A is greater.
○ Quantity B is greater.
○ The two quantities are equal.
○ The relationship cannot be determined from the information given.

2.

Quantity A	Quantity B
The percent increase from 5 to 4	The percent decrease from 5 to 4

○ Quantity A is greater.
○ Quantity B is greater.
○ The two quantities are equal.
○ The relationship cannot be determined from the information given.

3.

Quantity A	Quantity B
The circumference of a circular region with radius r	The perimeter of a square with side r

○ Quantity A is greater.
○ Quantity B is greater.
○ The two quantities are equal.
○ The relationship cannot be determined from the information given.

4.   <u>Quantity A</u>   <u>Quantity B</u>

The average   The average
(arithmetic mean)   (arithmetic mean) of
of 7, 3, 4, and 2 $2a + 5$, $4a$, and $7 - 6a$

○ Quantity A is greater.

○ Quantity B is greater.

○ The two quantities are equal.

○ The relationship cannot be determined from
    the information given.

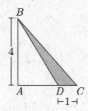

5.   <u>Quantity A</u>   <u>Quantity B</u>

The area of the $1\dfrac{1}{3}$
shaded region in ABC
divided by the area of
the unshaded region
in ABC

Triangle *ABC* is isosceles.

○ Quantity A is greater.

○ Quantity B is greater.

○ The two quantities are equal.

○ The relationship cannot be determined from
    the information given.

6. **Quantity A**   **Quantity B**

$3^{17} + 3^{18}$ $(4)3^{17}$

○ Quantity A is greater.
○ Quantity B is greater.
○ The two quantities are equal.
○ The relationship cannot be determined from the information given.

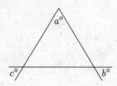

7. **Quantity A**   **Quantity B**

$b + c$ $180 - a$

○ Quantity A is greater.
○ Quantity B is greater.
○ The two quantities are equal.
○ The relationship cannot be determined from the information given.

8. If the cost of a one-hour telephone call is $7.20, what would be the cost of a ten-minute telephone call at the same rate?
   ○ $7.10
   ○ $3.60
   ○ $1.80
   ○ $1.20
   ○ $0.72

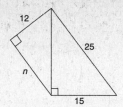

9. What is the value of *n* in the figure above?
   - ○ 9
   - ○ 15
   - ○ 16
   - ○ $12\sqrt{3}$
   - ○ 20

10. If $x + y = z$ and $x = y$, then which of the following must be true?
    - ☐ $2x + 2y = 2z$
    - ☐ $x - y = 0$
    - ☐ $x - z = y - z$
    - ☐ $x = z$
    - ☐ $x - y = 2z$

11. A movie theater is 3 blocks due north of a super-market and a beauty parlor is 4 blocks due east of the movie theater. How many blocks long is the street that runs directly from the supermarket to the beauty parlor?
    - ○ 2.5
    - ○ 3
    - ○ 4
    - ○ 5
    - ○ 7

12. The units digit of a 2-digit number is 3 times the tens digit. If the digits are reversed, the resulting number is 36 more than the original number. What is the original number?

○ 13

○ 26

○ 36

○ 62

○ 93

13. A restaurant owner sold 2 dishes to each of his customers at $4 per dish. At the end of the day, he had taken in $180, which included $20 in tips. How many customers did he serve?

Questions 14–16 refer to the following charts.

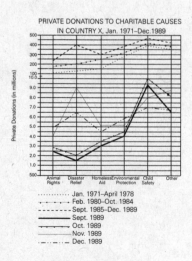

PRIVATE DONATIONS TO CHARITABLE CAUSES
IN COUNTRY X, Jan. 1971–Dec. 1989

Private Donations (in millions)

Animal Rights | Disaster Relief | Homeless Aid | Environmental Protection | Child Safety | Other

········· Jan. 1971–April 1978
─·─·─·─ Feb. 1980–Oct. 1984
─ ─ ─ ─ Sept. 1985–Dec. 1989
───── Sept. 1989
─┼─┼─ Oct. 1989
·········· Nov. 1989
─·─··─·─ Dec. 1989

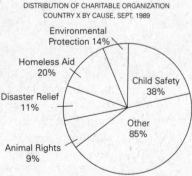

DISTRIBUTION OF CHARITABLE ORGANIZATION
COUNTRY X BY CAUSE, SEPT. 1989

Environmental Protection 14%

Homeless Aid 20%

Child Safety 38%

Disaster Relief 11%

Other 85%

Animal Rights 9%

Total = Charitable Organizations

14. Which of the following categories of charitable causes received the third-greatest amount in private donations from January 1971 to April 1978?
    ○ Disaster Relief
    ○ Homeless Aid
    ○ Environmental Protection
    ○ Child Safety
    ○ "Other" Causes

15. If funds contributed to child safety organizations in September 1989 were distributed evenly to those organizations, approximately how much did each charity receive?
    ○ $12,000,000
    ○ $9,400,000
    ○ $2,500,000
    ○ $250,000
    ○ $38,000

16. From September 1985 to December 1989, what was the approximate ratio of Private Donations, in millions, to Homeless Aid to Private Donations, in millions, to Animal Rights?
    ○ 20:9
    ○ 3:2
    ○ 4:3
    ○ 9:7
    ○ 5:6

17. Alex gave Jonathan *a* dollars. She gave Gina two dollars more than she gave Jonathan and she gave Louanne three dollars less than she gave Gina. In terms of *a*, how many dollars did Alex give Gina, Jonathan, and Louanne altogether?

   ○ $\dfrac{a}{3}$

   ○ $a - 1$

   ○ $3a$

   ○ $3a - 1$

   ○ $3a + 1$

18. If $m + n = p$, then $m^2 + 2mn + n^2 =$

   ○ $4p$

   ○ $np - m$

   ○ p^2

   ○ $p^2 + 4(m + p)$

   ○ $p^2 + np + m^2$

19. For all real numbers x and y, if $x * y = x(x - y)$, then $x * (x * y) =$

   ○ $x^2 - xy$

   ○ $x^2 - 2xy$

   ○ $x^3 - x^2 - xy$

   ○ $x^3 - (xy)^2$

   ○ $x^2 - x^3 + x^2y$

20. If x is an integer $1 < x < 10$, then which of the following could be the remainder when 117 is divided by x ?

   ☐ 1

   ☐ 2

   ☐ 3

   ☐ 4

   ☐ 5

   ☐ 6

   ☐ 7

PART **IV**

ANSWERS AND
EXPLANATIONS

VERBAL DRILL 1

1. **D**   The clue in the sentence is "Children . . . have become 'hasty viewers.'" The trigger punctuation is a "same-direction" semicolon. So a good word for the blank would be "wanders." In any case, it has to be a negative word. The words in answer choices (A), (B), and (E) are positive, and answer choice (C) isn't really negative. That leaves (D).

2. **C**   Find the story. This architect doesn't promote himself, therefore his fame can't be a result of self promotion. Try a word like fame for the blank. Neither *proficiency* nor *temperament* mean fame so cross off choices (A) and (B). *Prominence* could work, so give (C) a maybe and move on. There is nothing in the sentence to indicate that the architect is superior, so eliminate choice (D). While the architect may have been reticent, we are looking for fame. Cross off choice (E). The best answer is (D).

3. **virtuosic, mellifluous**

    The clue "roused the audience to a standing ovation" indicates that both blanks need a positive word. The toughest part about filling either blank is the difficult vocab in the two columns. Use positive/negative to eliminate unlikely choices. *Hackneyed* sounds negative, while *virtuosic* looks a lot like virtue, a positive word. In the second column, *mellifluous* looks a bit like mellow, which is usually a good thing, but *insipid* has the prefix in, which means against. That may give it a negative connotation. All told, *virtuosic* and *mellifluous* both have positive meanings and suit the sentence best.

4. **ambiguous, dissuade**

    The clue for the first blank, "such unproven programs," comes at the end of the sentence. You need a word meaning inconclusive to describe the results. *Conclusive* is clearly the opposite of what you want, but *ambiguous* looks good, especially given its prefix ambi, which means "going in both directions." *Auspicious*, in contrast, may sound like suspicious, but if you've been studying your Hit Parade, you'll know that it has a positive meaning. Hang onto *ambiguous* and work the second blank. You already know that the program's results have not been proven, but the reverse-direction trigger however indicates that those findings are having an unexpected or contradictory effect on parents' desire to enroll their children. Since the phrase "have failed to" comes right before the blank, you need a word meaning discourage. Keep *disabuse* and *dissuade* if you're not sure of their meanings, but get rid of distinguish. Meanwhile, notice that *dissuade* shares the same word root as persuade, but has the prefix dis, which means not. That makes it a likely choice, leaving *ambiguous* and *dissuade* as the two best answers.

5. **bliss, irrational, scant**

The reverse-direction trigger nonetheless tells you that the first blank needs a word meaning the opposite of either "rational" or "pragmatic". Since there's no synonym for irrational in the first column, try not practical and use POE. While an impractical person might make his own suffering a priority—via *melancholy* or *discord*—*bliss* makes more sense, especially given that "regard for their own happiness" is mentioned later in the sentence. Another reverse-direction trigger, in contrast, is also used to reverse either rational or pragmatic for the second blank. Choose *irrational* from the second column and work the third blank. The first part of the sentence tells you that classical economics sees humans as trying to maximize their own happiness, and then the reverse-direction trigger in contrast gives us Veblen's view. As such, the third blank needs a word that means the opposite of maximizing happiness. *Scant* is the closest match from the third column, making it, *bliss*, and *irrational* the best answers.

6. **plagiarism, proliferate, ensure**

The clue at the end of the sentence, "copying from a website," gives us *plagiarism* for the first blank. Use the second part of the sentence and the reverse trigger "however" for the second blank; since their fears were not realized, we know we need a word like increase. If you don't know the word *proliferate*, studying your Greek roots can make it a great bet. For the last blank, we know that the educators are checking their students' work, so a good word for the last blank would be prove. *Rebut* is tempting, but doesn't quite fit, and *neglect* isn't even close, so we're left with *ensure*, the correct answer.

7. **E**   The conclusion of the argument is the first sentence—medieval stoneworkers are more skilled than modern ones—and the results of the survey provide the premise on which this conclusion is based. The argument assumes, though, that cathedrals are typical of medieval stonework; if not, the medieval masons are being evaluated on an atypical sample of their work. Thus, choice (E) most weakens the argument: If lower quality stonework is more likely to be destroyed, then medieval masons are being judged on their best work—their worst work likely having been destroyed long ago. Choices (A) and (B) would both strengthen the argument: choice (A), by removing a possible distinction between medieval and modern masons that might otherwise account for the difference in quality; choice (B), by directly supporting the above assumption. Without further information relating building size or apprenticeship length to skill in stonework, finally, both choices (C) and (D) are beyond the scope of the argument.

8. **C**   This is a main idea question about the passage as a whole. Your "treasure hunt" should have revealed that the passage is basically discussing the way in which Strachey interprets the English women's movement. Eliminate (B) right away because it's not about a "literary" work. Eliminate (D) because it's not a "novel analysis." Eliminate (A) and (E) because they are too specific. That leaves (C).

9. **C**   For line reference questions, go back to the lines cited, and read about five lines before and after those lines. You can find the answer in either place for this question. The first sentence of the paragraph tells us Strachey is writing about "the historical connections between the women's movement and other social and political developments." Choice (C) is just a paraphrase of this.

10. **B**   Look back in the passage for the place where the author "faults" Strachey. It's in the last paragraph, in lines 46–50. The author states, "Where Strachey pictured a relatively fixed image of domestic women throughout the first half of the nineteenth century, recent historical and literary works suggest that this image was both complex and unstable." Sounds like (B).

11. **D**   First, go back to the passage to find out what the author said about "the similarity between the English and American women's movements." It's at the end of the first paragraph. The

author says that "like its American counterpart, the English women's movement had a powerful sense of its own historic importance and of its relationship to wider social and political change." So you're looking for an answer choice that would indicate that was not true. Choice (D) directly contradicts the author's assertion.

12. **unrecognizable, reworked**

The best word for the blank here is something like "new" since we know that it is very different and we have the change direction trigger "though." The best two answers, therefore, are choices (B) and (E). None of the other choices really match each other or the meaning of the blank.

13. **furtive, surreptitious**

The clue for the blank is "he had ulterior motives." Think sneaky or secretive and use POE. *Inconspicuous* is out, since it's the opposite of the clue, but hang onto *furtive* (even if you don't know its meaning). *Overt* is also the opposite of sneaky; get rid of it. *Unorthodox* and *predictable*, meanwhile, don't match the clue, but *surreptitious* does. That leaves *furtive* and *surreptitious*, the two best answers.

14. **urbane, cosmopolitan**

Since the hotel had both "refined interiors" and an "amply stocked reading room", it would appeal to guests who were well-read and liked refinement. Think sophisticated or worldly and use POE. *Philistine* is the opposite of refined or worldly, but both *urbane* and *cosmopolitan* are solid matches. In contrast, *uncouth's* meaning is very similar to that of *philistine*, so cross out that choice. *Grandiloquent* and *pretentious*, meanwhile, don't match the clue, leaving you with *urbane* and *cosmopolitan*.

15. **amiable, affable**

"His inherent irascibility" is reversed by the change-direction trigger not, which comes before the blank describing Wilbert. You need a word that means the opposite of irascible. Think friendly or good-tempered and use POE. Neither *loquacious* nor *pedantic* means friendly, but *amiable* matches. *Garrulous*, meanwhile, has the same meaning as loquacious, so cross it out. Finally, *affable* is a good match but *stentorian* doesn't work. *Amiable* and *affable* suit the sentence best.

16.   It is hard from our modern perspective to imagine that theatre has the power to influence politics, yet the plays of pre-republican Ireland did just that.

> The passage starts out with its conclusion that, in the case of Ireland, theater influenced politics. The rest of the paragraph tells how this occurred.

17.   **C**   Go back to the first paragraph. In lines 7–8 the passage states, "In some localities the mosquito was abundant but malaria rare or absent."

18.   **C**   Try putting your own word in the passage to replace host. The trigger but indicates that the reference to distinct biological traits should contrast with the statement that the mosquitoes seem almost identical, so you need a word that means something like large number. Of the choices, *multitude* is the best match. Beware of choice (A), which, though tempting, refers specifically to people. Likewise, be careful with choice (E): while the mosquitoes in question do, in fact, support parasites, that usage wouldn't make sense in this context.

19.   **A**   Reread the second sentence of the second paragraph. It says that the mosquito becomes a carrier when it feeds on human blood.

20.   **E**   Choice (E) is best supported in the passage. The first paragraph discusses a seemingly inconsistent relationship between the presence of the mosquitoes and the prevalence of malaria, a paradox resolved by the discovery of multiple species among the insects; the boldface text suggests why this multiplicity of species wasn't immediately apparent. Choices (C) and (D), while appropriately referring to the paradox, incorrectly describe the value of the bolded text: it neither resolves nor clarifies the importance of that paradox. Choices (A) and (B), finally, are not supported because the boldface text doesn't directly weaken or strengthen the author's main point, which is the discussion of one important step in the effort to eradicate malaria.

VERBAL DRILL #2

1. **C**   That semicolon is a trigger punctuation. It tells you that the first part of the sentence agrees with the second part. The second part contains the clue "what one group sees as peace-keeping, another group might see as subjugation." How can we describe that—it sounds like a contradiction. How about "contradictory" for the blank? Time to go to the answers. You can eliminate (A) *academic*, because it doesn't mean contradictory. Choice (B) *portentous* means predicting the future, which might be true of historical events, but has nothing to do with this sentence. Choice (C) *paradoxical* means seemingly contradictory, so keep it (if you weren't sure, you'd keep it in anyway). Choice (D) *trifling* means frivolous or of little value, so eliminate it. Choice (E) *bellicose* means warlike, which might be true of some historical events, but has nothing to do with this sentence. The best answer is (C).

2. **B**   The clue for the blank after the trigger word "however" is "daily routines," so the word in the blank can be "routine." That definitely eliminates (A), (D), and (E). If you know what *quotidian* or *recalcitrant* means, you know the answer is (B). If you don't, (C) is a good guess (although it's wrong).

3. **fledgling, precipitously**

    The only thing that we really know about the store is that it is pretty new, so that would be a good word for the first blank. While *urbane* and *ostentatious* could both apply to a clothing store, they do not match the meaning of the clue. Since we know that the situation is a crisis, a good word for the second blank would be something like a lot. The best answer, then, is *precipitously* while none of the other choices match the direction of the clue.

4. **abstruse, lucid**

    What would earn Reagan the distinction of "The Great Communicator," other than an ability to make difficult or complicated topics easy to understand? Hang onto *abstruse*, but don't fall for the trap of *obtuse*. You can also cross out *mundane*, as it means common or ordinary—not complicated. Moving to the second blank, think clear or understandable, given the first part of the sentence. *Palatable* is close, but *lucid* is a much more precise match. *Munificent*, meanwhile, doesn't mean understandable, making *abstruse* and *lucid* the best choices.

5. **arduous, transient, static**

"Is made even more difficult" is the clue for the first blank. Recycle difficult and use POE. Only *arduous* matches. Regarding the second blank, the clue "people seldom reside in any one place for very long" suggests a word meaning moving around or mobile. *Inert* is the opposite of the clue, and *aesthetic* doesn't match, so choose *transient* and work the third blank. The change-direction trigger however, which comes right after the blank, calls for a word meaning the opposite of mobile. *Static* is a strong match, making it, *arduous*, and *transient* the best choices.

6. **bedlam, epithets, neophyte**

The second and third blanks might be a little easier on this one. A good word for the third blank would be something like inexperienced since we are told that a person with "more experience" would have handled things better. The best choice, then, is answer *neophyte*. For the second blank, a good word would be something like insults since we are told that things were getting personal. The best answer here is *epithets*. For the first blank a good word would be something like chaos since the meeting started out well but resulted in disarray. The best answer here is *bedlam*.

7. **B**   The examples of how different terminology can determine who benefits is an example of the issues that make selling naming rights so legally complicated, choice (B). The naming rights may be complicated, but they are not described as confusing, choice (A). Answer choice (C) draws too large a conclusion from a specific example. Answer choice (D) is too extreme for the situation described. The differences in benefits are between facility owners and teams; the terminology does not affect the community's benefits (E). Therefore, the best answer is (B).

8. **B**   In the credited response, the author suggests that the naming rights may seem like a win-win proposition. However, the rest of the sentence—and the rest of the paragraph—is devoted to enumerating some of the difficulties and concerns that such deals often raise.

9. **D**   Try putting your own word in the passage to replace practice. The trigger though indicates that the first part of the sentence will contrast with the current proliferation of sponsorships, so a word like activity or deed might make sense—anything that conveys the meaning that it was once unheard of for something to happen. Of the choices, action is the best fit.

10. **C**   Choice (A) is not supported, as the passage makes no mention of other playwrights to whom a comparison can be made. Choice (B) is also not supported: the focus here is on a wartime comedy with a serious message, but the author doesn't comment on the propriety of studying this or any other play. Choice (C) is supported by the main idea of the passage, that Lysistrata has an oft-overlooked meaning that depends on the political situation in Greece at the time of its composition.

11. **B**   Choice (B) is best supported by the passage: the oracle is brought up in a list of examples supporting the importance of the idea of Greek unity in the play. Choices (A) and (C) can be eliminated because the passage doesn't directly relate the oracle to Lampito or the origin of the conspiracy. Choice (D) is also not supported: although a superficial interpretation of Lysistrata is being questioned, the passage doesn't provide enough information to characterize either interpretation as earlier. Choice (E), finally, is backwards, as the oracle supports the author's emphasis on cohesion in the play.

12. **A**   The conclusion of the argument is at the end: "Significant progress is being made toward the extending the lives of cancer patients." The premise on which the argument is based is that patients are living longer after their initial diagnosis. For this argument to be valid, though, you need to assume that length of life is the same thing as time after initial diagnosis. Hence, choice (A) is the best response: if cancer is being diagnosed progressively earlier, then people could be aware of their condition longer without living any longer. Keep a close eye on the scope of the argument to help you eliminate the incorrect choices. The argument isn't about a comparison among types of cancer, or between cancer and other diseases, so eliminate choices (B) and (E). Likewise, the argument isn't about the number of either cancer diagnoses or people who make full recoveries, so eliminate choices (C) and (D).

13. **congruence, concurrence**

> "Fervent schisms...were largely overplayed" is the clue indicating that the blank needs a word meaning the opposite of disagreement. Think agreement and use POE. *Congruence* matches, but *asperity* and *contradiction* go in the opposite direction of agreement. *Concurrence*, like *congruence*, matches the clue, but *impassivity* and *truculence*, like the second and third choices, go in the opposite direction of the clue. That leaves *congruence* and *concurrence* as the two best answers.

14. **mettle, tenacity**

> The blank needs a word meaning perseverance or determination, given the semicolon, which acts as a same-direction trigger, followed by the rest of the sentence, which discusses all that Johnson achieved "though he never attended school." *Mettle* works, but *timidity* does not. *Tenacity*, like mettle, is a good match for perseverance, but *tenuousness* goes in the opposite direction. Apply your clue word to the two remaining choices. Does *candor* mean perseverance? What about *alacrity*? Neither one matches, leaving you with *mettle* and *tenacity*, the two best answers.

15. **officious, meddlesome**

> What does the sentence tell you about the sales clerk? From the clue "drove many a potential customer away with her pushy, overeager manner," you can recycle pushy or overeager for the blank and use POE. Eliminate *loquacious* and *irreverent* if you know what they mean (here's where knowing your vocab comes in handy). *Officious*, on the other hand, could work, but *innocuous* doesn't mean anything close to pushy, so cross it out. *Meddlesome*, like *officious*, matches the clue, but *vigilant* doesn't mean pushy or overeager. That leaves you with *officious* and *meddlesome*, which are the two best choices.

16. **complaisance, deference**

> The clue for the blank is "even the most compliant of employees." Recycle part of the clue word and apply compliancy to the answer choices. *Effrontery* and *truculence* go in the opposite direction of compliancy, so toss those two. *Deference* makes sense (think defer), but cross out both *prevarication* and *chicanery*, since they have to do with dishonesty (don't let the phrase

"motivated by a hidden agenda" shift your focus away from the clue for the blank, which describes compliant employees). *Complaisance*, in contrast, agrees with the clue, making it and *deference* the two best choices.

17. **C**   The first sentence of the passage says that dopamine is recycled to prevent overstimulation. This clue tells you that released dopamine must have a stimulating effect, so pique means stimulate. Neither choice (A) nor (D) has this meaning. Choice (E) specifies a negative stimulation, which is not supported by the text. Choice (B) is also not supported by context. *Excite* is a good synonym for stimulate and is the correct choice.

18. **D**   Choice (A) is not supported by the text because the discovery of a different process does not necessarily make the old one incorrect. The same logic applies when considering choice (B); that one method is traditional does not make a different one incorrect. The passage never gives any indication of preferences or personal beliefs, so choice (C) is also incorrect. Choice (E) goes too far in saying that many people cannot overcome addiction; the passage does not offer statistics on recovery. Choice (D) is correct because the first sentence indicates a long standing belief in DAT blockage as the primary problem.

19. **C**   Choice (A) is not supported: the passage suggests that the manageable distance for oxen was less than that for horses, but no specifics are provided for either animal. Choice (B) is also not supported, as the passage focuses on agricultural developments; the military preeminence of mounted cavalry is only mentioned as inspiring early selective breeding. Choice (C), finally, is supported by the passage: the first paragraph indicates that the neck strap of the older harnesses inhibited the flow of both air and blood to the horse's brain.

20. **B**   Choice (B) is best supported: the passage discusses the move to horses as primary draft animals, and the boldface text gives factors that hindered that transition. Choices (A) and (C), then, both contradict the passage and can be eliminated. Choices (D) and (E) are also not supported by the passage. Although the factors in boldface might be considered part of a paradox—how horses overtook oxen despite significant disadvantages—the information presented neither solves nor further explores the ramifications of any such paradox.

MATH DRILL #1

1. **A**   In a parallelogram, opposite angles are equal, and the big angle plus the small angle adds up to 180 degrees. So $x + 120 = 180$. That makes Quantity A 60, which is bigger than the 45 in Quantity B. The answer is (A).

2. **A**   To find the amount Mr. Jones paid in addition to the regular price of the bedroom set, multiply $69 by the 9 months and get $621. Then add the $300 payment. $621 + 300 = 921$. So Mr. Jones paid an additional $921. The $23 in Quantity A is larger than the $21 in Quantity B. The answer is (A).

3. **B**   To find the perimeter of triangle BCD, first, find the length of BD using the Pythagorean theorem. $5^2 + BD^2 = 13^2$. Or you may remember that $5^2 + 12^2 = 13^2$. So $BD = 12$. Then, you can find the third side of triangle BCD. $12^2 + DC^2 = 15^2$. Notice that this is a 3:4:5 right triangle. So DC is 9. Next, add up the sides of triangle BCD. $9 + 12 + 15 = 36$. So, Quantity A is 36. Because Quantity B is 42, (B) is the answer.

4. **B**   Draw yourself a picture! The formula for circumference is $C = \pi d$, also known as $2\pi r$. Because $r = \frac{1}{2}$, $C = (2)\pi \left(\frac{1}{2}\right)$, or π. So you have π in Quantity A and 4 in Quantity B. Remember that π is equal to a little more than 3. That means the answer is (B).

5. **D**   First, Plug In an easy number. How about $x = 2$? That gives us 3 as the quantity in Quantity A and –1 as the quantity in Quantity B. We know that 3 is greater than –1; *so far* the answer is (A). Eliminate (B) and (C) on your scratch paper. For our second round of Plugging In, try $x = 0$. That gives us 1 in Quantity A and 1 in Quantity B—now the two columns are equal. You Plugged In *different* numbers, you got *different* answers. Therefore, the answer is (D).

6. **B**   When you see the word "average," make your pie. In this case, you have the average, 17, and the number, 2. That makes the total 34. In other words, the two numbers have to add up to 34, but neither of them can be 12 or less.

Because Quantity A is asking for twice the larger of the two integers, figure out what the largest integer could be by pairing it with the smallest integer we can use, or 13. If the total is 34, and one number is 13, that means the other number is 21 because 21 + 13 = 34. So, in Quantity A, we get 42, which is twice 21. We have 44 in Quantity B, so (B) is the answer.

7. **D**   First, Plug In a pair of easy numbers. Try 3 for x and 4 for y. (4 is a good plug-in for y, because $\sqrt{4}$ is an integer.) This gives 12 for Quantity A and 6 for Quantity B. With these plug-ins, choice (A) works, which means you can eliminate choices (B) and (C). But you have to plug in again, because you still have choice (D) to contend with. Plug In some weird numbers. How about 0 for x and 0 for y? (There's no rule that says x and y have to be different.) That gives 0 for Quantity A and 0 for Quantity B. Because these numbers make the two columns equal, this proves that Quantity A is not always the answer, and the correct answer is (D).

8. **B**   First, there were no variables in this problem, so the answer can't be (D). The word "inclusive" in Quantity B is the key. "Inclusive" means including 15 and –15 and 0, which must be more than 30 (in Quantity A). You'll prove it by listing them: –15, –14, –13, –12, –11, –10, –9, –8, –7, –6, –5, –4, –3, –2, –1, 0, 1, 2, 3, 4, 5, 6, 7, 8, 9, 10, 11, 12, 13, 14, 15. That's 31, and that's (B).

9. **D**   Which costs more, the car or the paint job? The car. What do the answer choices represent? The cost of the car. Ballpark first. If the combined cost was $4,800, and the biggest chunk of that is the cost of the car, choices (A) and (B), are ridiculously low. A $4,000 paint job for an $800 car? No way. Eliminate those choices. What choices are left? (C), (D), and (E). Start plugging in the middle of those values, (D), $4,000. Hey, it's also the easiest number to work with, so why not? You're told that the cost of the paint job was $\frac{1}{5}$ the cost of the car. One-fifth of $4,000 is $800 (now you see where that trap answer choice came from). Is $4,000 plus $800 equal to $4,800? Yes. You're done—the answer is (D).

10. **B**   To find the perimeter of the figure, you need to add up all the sides. To find the missing side of the rectangle, solve for the opposite side of the rectangle, using the Pythagorean theorem: $a^2 + b^2 = c^2$. You may remember that $5^2 + 12^2 = 13^2$. So the missing sides of the rectangle are each 13. Now, add up the sides of the figure: $5 + 12 + 17 + 13 + 17 = 64$. That's (B).

11. **A**   Plug In 2 for x and 3 for y—that makes xy an even integer.

   (A) $(2)(3) + 5 = 11$. That's odd, so leave it in.

   (B) $2 + 3 = 5$. That's odd, so leave it in.

   (C) $\dfrac{2}{3}$. That's not an integer, so eliminate it.

   (D) $4(2) = 8$. That's even, so eliminate it.

   (E) $7(2)(3) = 42$. That's even, so eliminate it.

   So, you got rid of choices (C), (D), and (E). But standard operating procedure on a "must be" question says we need to Plug In twice; otherwise, how would we choose between (A) and (B)? At first, you made x even and y odd. Make them both even and just change y to 4. Is xy even, using these numbers? Yes, it's 8. Go back to the two remaining choices.

   (A) $(2)(3) + 5 = 13$. That's still odd, so leave it in.
   (B) $2 + 4 = 6$. That's even, so eliminate it. The answer is (A).

12. **25**   Don't solve for x: you're told that $3x = -2$, so substitute -2 for $3x$ in the problem to yield $(-2 - 3)^2$, or $(-5)^2$, which equals 25.

13. **A**   A line has 180 degrees, so $a + 20 + b = 180$. That means that $a + b = 160$. You're also told that $a = 3b$. So, plug in those answer choices for b: (C) $b = 25$, so $a = 75$. Does $25 + 75 = 160$? Nope, it's 100, too small. (B) $b = 30$, so $a = 90$. Does $30 + 90 = 160$? Nope, it's 120, too small. Bet the answer's (A). Double-check to make sure. (A) $b = 40$, so $a = 120$. Does $40 + 120 = 160$? Yes. That's the answer.

14. **8,230**   First, add the total number of male and female voters to get the overall total of 9,053. Don't subtract 10% from that, though—that's a 10% decrease, and the big trap in the

problem. Instead, find the number that gives 9,053 when increased by 10%. Increasing something by 10% makes it 110% of its original value, so translate the question "9,053 is 110% of what?" into the equation $9,053 = x$. Solve for x, and $x = 8,230$.

15. D Take advantage of the work that's already done for you— the total number of females—and add the males who were less than 48 years old: $4,671 + 1,030 + 1,114 = 6,815$.

16. C You can compare the ratio of the actual numbers of people, or the ratio of the percentages. Either way the ratios will be the same. Since we already know the percentage of Democrats and the percentages are smaller numbers, let's stay with percentages. To find out the percentage of male voters age 48 to 62, write "1,291 is what percent of 9,053?" as an equation on your scratch paper: $1,291 = x/100(9,053)$. The answer is 14.2%. The ratio of 43% to 14% is closest to 3 to 1. The correct answer is (C).

17. C Use those answer choices! Because the question is asking for the least number, start by Plugging In (A), the least number in the answer choices.
  (A) Does $\{3(-3) + 2\} \{-3 - 3\} = 0$? $(-7)(-6) = -42$, which isn't 0.
  (B) Does $\{3(-2) + 2\} \{-2 - 2\} = 0$? $(-4)(-4) = -16$, which isn't 0.
  (C) Does $\{3(-\frac{2}{3}) + 2\} \{-\frac{2}{3} - 3\} = 0$? $(0)(-3\frac{2}{3}) = 0$. Bingo!

18. 236 Draw yourself a picture! To find the perimeter of a rectangle, you need to know the length and the width. If the newspaper ad with a width of 14 has the same area as another ad 52 long and 28 wide, that means that 14(length) = 52(28). Divide both sides by 14, and you get length = 52(2) = 104. So, the perimeter of the mystery ad is $104 + 104 + 14 + 14$, which equals 236.

19. C With all of these percents, wouldn't it be nice to have a total number? Just Plug In one. Make the total number of voters 100 (the best number to plug in when you're dealing with percents). 60 percent of the voters are women, so that's 60 women, and the remaining voters are men, so that's 40 (we made the total 100, remember?) men. 30 percent of the women would be 30 percent of 60, which is $\frac{30}{100}$ (60), or 18 women, who voted for candidate X. 20 percent of the men would be 20 percent of 40, which is $\frac{20}{100}$ (40), or 8 men, who voted for candidate X. So, the total number of people voting for candidate X is 18 + 8, or 26. Because your total is 100, 26 is equal to 26 percent. That's (C).

20. **B, C,** and **E**

Use your on-screen calculator to find 21 × 54 × 22, and Plug In The Answers to see which ones divide into integers. Alternately, you could work with the factors: 21 = 7 × 3, 54 = 3 × 3 × 3 × 2, and 22 = 2 × 11, so you can divide their product by any number that contains only the factors in 22 × 34 × 7 × 11. The denominators in choices (A) and (F) both have 5 as factors, and choice (D) has too many 2's; the rest of the choices all yield integers.

MATH DRILL #2

1. **A**   When in doubt, expand it out, and don't calculate, because this is quant comp and you only have to compare. In Quantity A, there is (4)(2)(2)(2)(2)(2)(2). In Quantity B, there is (6)(4)(4). Break it down even further: Quantity A is (2)(2)(2)(2)(2)(2)(2)(2), and Quantity B is (3)(2)(2)(2)(2)(2). Now, get rid of anything both columns have in common. Each column has five 2's, so cross them out. What's left? (2)(2)(2) in Quantity A and (3) in Quantity B. In other words, Quantity A has an 8, and Quantity B has a 3. The answer is (A).

2. **A**   First of all, there are only numbers in this problem, so the answer cannot be (D). Now, the formula for percent increase is the difference divided by the original, multiplied by 100. In Quantity A, the difference (between 4 and 5) is 1, and the original number is 4, so that's $\frac{1}{4}$. Multiply that by 100 and you get 25%. In Quantity B, the difference (between 4 and 5) is 1, but the original number is 5, so that's $\frac{1}{5}$. Multiply that by 100 and you get 20%. 25% is bigger than 20%, so the answer is (A).

3. A   Draw yourself a picture! Plug In some numbers and see what happens. To start with, make $r = 2$. Then, you get $2\pi r = 4\pi$ (which is about 12-ish) in Quantity A and $4(2) = 8$ in Quantity B. So Quantity A is greater if $r = 2$. Eliminate choices (B) and (C). Now Plug In a weird number; make $r = \frac{1}{2}$. Then you get π in Quantity A and 2 in Quantity B. Quantity A wins again. You can't Plug In 0 or a negative number because r is the radius of the circle and the side of the square. The answer is (A).

4. C   When you see the word "average," draw a pie. In Quantity A, the average is $7 + 3 + 4 + 2$, or 16, divided by 4, which is 4. In Quantity B, you have to find the average of $2a + 5$, $4a$, and $7 - 6a$. Why not Plug In something for a to make this easier? How about 2? Now you're finding the average of 9, 8, and –5. $9 + 8 - 5 = 12$, divided by the number of numbers, which is 3, gives 4. So far the answer is (C). Plug In again— something weird this time, just to be sure. How about 0? Now you're finding the average of 5, 0, and 7. 12 divided by the number of numbers, which is 3, gives 4. Again, you get (C). By the way, you could also have solved Quantity B by adding everything up as is: $2a + 5 + 4a + 7 - 6a = 12$. 12 divided by the number of numbers, which is 3, gives 4.

5. C   Triangle ABC is isosceles. That means that the base and the height are each equal to 4. So the base of the unshaded region is 3, because the base of the shaded region is 1. The area of triangle ABC is $\frac{1}{2}(4)(4)$, or 8. The area of triangle ABD is $\frac{1}{2}(4)(3)$, or 6. Subtract the area of ABD from the area of ABC to get the area of the shaded region, BCD. That's $8 - 6$, which is 2. So, in Quantity A, the area of the shaded region, 2, divided by the area of the unshaded region, 6, is $\frac{2}{6}$, or $\frac{1}{3}$. The answer is (C).

6. C   Looks ugly, doesn't it? This is a tough one, but don't worry; you'd never be expected to calculate these. All you need to do is compare. Start by doing a little factoring to change the look of these numbers. In Quantity A, what's the biggest thing that we can "pull out" of 3^{17} and 3^{18}? You can divide the whole thing, or "pull out" 3^{17}, so you end up with $3^{17}(1 + 3^1)$, or $3^{17}(4)$. Looks like Quantity B, doesn't it? The answer is (C).

7. **C**   Don't forget to Plug In on geometry problems with variables. Plugging In according to the rule of 180, You can make $a = 50$, and make the other two angles inside the triangle 60 and 70. Because b and c are vertical to the other angles in the triangle, $b + c = 130$ in Quantity A. $180 - 50 = 130$ in Quantity B. The answer is (C).

8. **D**   First of all, do a little Ballparking. If a one-hour call costs $7.20, a ten-minute call must cost much less. Eliminate (A). Now, make a proportion, but first, change "one hour" into "60 minutes," because you're comparing it to ten minutes. So, you have: $\dfrac{\text{cost}}{\text{minutes}} = \dfrac{7.20}{60} = \dfrac{x}{10}$. A little cross-multiplying gets you $60x = (7.20)(10)$, or $60x = 72$. Divide both sides by 60 and you get $x = 1.20$. That's (D).

9. **C**   To find the value of n, start with the right triangle for which you're given two of the three sides. Use the Pythagorean theorem: $15^2 + b^2 = 25^2$. Notice that this is a 3:4:5 right triangle; $15 = 3(5)$ and $25 = 5(5)$. So $b = 20$ or $4(5)$. Now you have two of the three sides of the triangle: $12^2 + n^2 = 20$. Notice that you've got another 3:4:5 right triangle. $12 = 3(4)$ and $20 = 5(4)$. So $n = 4(4)$ or 16. That's (C).

10. **A, B, C, and D**

The minute you see the phrase "must be" you know you need to Plug In more than once and you are going to use your "must be" set-up. On your scratch paper, list your answer choices down the left, and $x =$, $y =$, and $z =$ three times across the top. Now Plug In according to the rules you've been given. If $x = 2$ then $y = 2$ and z must equal 4. Check your answer choices. For (A), $4 + 4 = 8$. This works, give it a check. For (B), $2 - 2 = 0$, this works, give it a check. For (C), $2 - 4 = 2 - 4$, this works, give it a check. For (D), $2 = \dfrac{4}{2}$, this works, give it a check. And for (E), $2 - 2 = 8$. This does not work, so cross off answer choice (E). You are going to have to Plug In more than once, but that is what your set-up is for. Make sure you try all of the weird numbers, so plug in fractions, negative numbers, and zero. You will find that (A), (B), (C), and (D) will work all of the time. Since this is an All That Apply question, the correct answer is (A), (B), (C), and (D).

11. **D** Remember, if you don't get a diagram, draw one yourself. Your little map should form a 3:4:5 right triangle, so the street from the supermarket to the beauty parlor is 5 blocks long. Drawing your own diagram makes this problem so much easier!

12. **B** Plug In those answer choices! There are two conditions on the answer. First, its second digit must be 3 times the first digit. Because ETS's answer must satisfy both conditions, you can eliminate any choice that fails to satisfy either of them. Therefore, you tackle one condition at a time. Choice (C): Is 6 three times 3? No. Eliminate. Choice (B): Is 6 three times 2? Yes. A possibility. Choice (D): Is 2 three times 6? No. Eliminate. Choice (A): Is 3 three times 1? Yes. A possibility. Choice (E): Is 3 three times 9? No. Eliminate. You've already narrowed it down to two possibilities, choices (A) and (B). Now you apply the second condition, that the reversed form of the number must be 36 more than the original number. Check the remaining choices: Choice (A): Is 31 equal to 36 more than 13? No. Eliminate. That's it, the answer must be (B). Check it to make sure: 62 *is* exactly 36 more than 26.

13. **20** The information about tips is the catch. Its only purpose is to cause careless errors. Confront this trap by reducing the day's total by $20—to $160. Now you're left with a very straightforward problem. If each customer bought two $4 dishes, then each customer spent $8 total, and $160 ÷ $8 = 20.

14. **C** Go to the graph and find January 1971 to April 1978. Use Process of Elimination. The greatest amount of private donations to charitable causes for that period was to the category of Child Safety. Eliminate (D). The second greatest was Other. Eliminate choice (E). The third greatest was Environmental Protection. That's (C).

15. D This question requires you to find the amount of money received by Child Safety organizations in September 1989 from the left-hand chart. It was $9.4 million. Then, divide that amount by the number of Child Safety organizations—38 (from the right-hand chart). It's time to Ballpark! To make it as easy as possible, round both of those figures up. Pretend it's $10 million divided by 40. That's $250,000. That's (D).

16. C Go to the graph and find September 1985 to December 1989. The amount donated to Homeless Aid causes for that period was about $300 million. The amount donated to Animal Rights causes for that period was about $225 million. You can reduce ratios! The ratio of 300:225 reduces to 12:9, or 4:3. That's (C).

17. E Plug In a number for a. How about 10? So, Alex gave Jonathan 10 dollars. She gave Gina two dollars more than she gave Jonathan, so she gave Gina 12 dollars. She gave Louanne three dollars less than she gave Gina, so she gave Louanne 9 dollars. So altogether, Alex gave Gina, Jonathan, and Louanne 10 + 12 + 9, or 31 dollars. (By the way, just ignore that "in terms of a." Because you Plugged In, you're not answering the question in terms of a anymore.) Now check the answers, Plugging In 10 for a, and looking for the target answer, 31.

(A) Does $\dfrac{10}{3}$ = 31? Nope.

(B) Does $10 - 1 = 31$? Nope.

(C) Does $3(10) = 31$? Nope.

(D) Does $3(10) - 1 = 31$? Nope.

(E) Does $3(10) + 1 = 31$? Yes. The answer is (E).

18. C Remember those quadratic equations? Doesn't $m^2 + 2mn + n^2$ look exactly like $x^2 + 2xy + y^2$, which equals $(x + y)^2$? That means you could rewrite $m^2 + 2mn + n^2$ as $(m + n)^2$. Now, you're also told that $m + n = p$, which means that p and $m + n$ are interchangeable. If you replace the $m + n$ in the $(m + n)^2$ with the p, you get p^2.

So, $m^2 + 2mn + n^2 = (m + n)^2 = p^2$. That's (C). Whew! But hey—you can also plug in on this one: 2 for m, 3 for n, and 5 for p—we get $2^2 + (2)(2)(3) + 3^2$, which equals 25. That's our target answer. Now, to the answers.

(A) $(4)(5) = 20$. Eliminate.

(B) $15 - 2 = 13$. Eliminate.

(C) $(5)^2 = 25$. Bingo!

(D) $(5)^2 + 4(2 + 5) = 25 + 28 = 53$. Eliminate.

(E) $(5)^2 + (3)(5) + (2)^2 = 25 + 15 + 4 = 44$. Eliminate.

It's (C)!

19. **E** Don't worry, there's no such thing as a "*." This is one of those funny-symboled function problems. This time, you don't have numbers to use. Sounds like a plug in! Plug In $x = 3$ and $y = 2$. First, you'll do the $x \approx y$ in the parentheses. You know that $x * y = x(x - y)$, so $3(3 - 2) = 3(1) = 3$. So, $x * (x * y)$ can be rewritten as $x * 3$. Now, remembering that you made $x = 3$, the question really is $3 * 3 = 3(3 - 3) = 3(0) = 0$. That's the target you're looking for in the answer choices: 0. So, Plug In $x = 3$ and $y = 2$ in the answer choices, and look for 0.

(A) Does $x^2 - xy = 0$? $(3)^2 - (3)(2) = 9 - 6 = 3$. Nope.

(B) Does $x^2 - 2xy = 0$? $(3)^2 - 2(3)(2) = 9 - 12 = -3$. Nope.

(C) Does $x^3 - x^2 - xy = 0$? $(3)^3 - (3)^2 - (3)(2) = 27 - 9 - 6 = 12$. Nope.

(D) Does $x^3 - (xy)^2 = 0$? $(3)^3 - \{(3)(2)\}^2 = 27 - 36 = -9$. Nope.

(E) Does $x^2 - x^3 + x^2y = 0$? $(3)^2 - (3)^3 + \{(3)^2(2)\} = 9 - 27 + 18 = 0$. Bingo!

20. **A, B, C, and E**

Just start dividing and find your remainders. $117 \div 2 = 58$ with a remainder of 1, so select choice (A). 117 is divisible by 3, so 3 doesn't give you a new remainder. $117 \div 4 = 29$ with a remainder of 1, but you already have 1. $117 \div 5 = 23$ with a remainder of 2, so select choice (B). $117 \div 6 = 19$ with a remainder of 3, so select choice (C). $117 \div 7 = 16$ with a remainder of 5, so select choice (E). $117 \div 8 = 14$ with a remainder of 5, but you already have 5. 117 is divisible by 9, so 9 doesn't give you a new remainder. The correct choices are (A), (B), (C), and (E).

 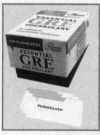